PSYCHOLOGY OF CONFUSION

A journey from **chaos** to **clarity**

DEEP TRIVEDI

Bestselling Author of I am The Mind, I am Gita, I am Krishna & Everything is Psychology

Also available in Hindi and Gujarati

DEEP TRIVEDI The Speaker

Deep Trivedi uses a unique combination of psycho-spiritual content, voice, language and expression, which effectuates an instantaneous transformation in his viewers and listeners. Millions of lives have been transformed just by listening to him.

His interactive workshops have brought about a revolutionary transformation in people's lives by addressing their day-to-day concerns. Deep Trivedi sheds light on every aspect of human life and mind and has extensively spoken on the Bhagavad Gita, Tao Te Ching, Ashtavakra Gita, Secrets of Nature, Mind, Soul, Time, Destiny, and numerous other topics such as:

- **Ego**
- **God**
- **Guilt**
- **Love**
- **Anger**
- **Future**
- **Wealth**
- **Phobias**
- **Religion**
- **Complex**
- **Marriage**
- **Freedom**
- **Partiality**
- **Day-Sleep**
- **DNA-Genes**
- **Path of Life**
- **Personality**
- **Expectation**
- **Acceptance**
- **Hypocrisy**
- **Creativity**
- **Confusion**
- **Good-Bad**
- **Involvement**
- **Concentration**
- **Laws of Nature**
- **Time and Space**
- **Mind and Brain**
- **Self-Confidence**
- **Joy and Happiness**
- **Natural Intelligence**
- **Power of Transformation**

Full workshop videos by Deep Trivedi on the above topics are available on **Deep Trivedi YouTube** channel

DEEP TRIVEDI

'Maximum Workshops on Psychological Aspects of Tao Te Ching', 'Maximum Workshops on Ashtavakra Gita' and 'Maximum Workshops on Bhagavad Gita', spanning 168 hours, 28 minutes, 50 seconds in 58 days in different national and international record books. He also holds the record for 'Maximum Number of Quotations on Human Life' (about 12038) on subjects such as Soul, Human Life, Psychology, Laws of Nature, Destiny and many more. He has also been awarded an Honorary Doctorate for his works on the psychology of Bhagavad Gita. His interactive workshops have brought about a revolutionary transformation in people's lives by addressing their day-to-day concerns. These workshops have been conducted in front of live audiences across India.

He is known for his special ability to touch upon the deepest aspects of life and explain them in simple language, leaving no scope for ambiguity. The distinct psychological-spiritual language and expression in his writings and workshops begin to have an instant effect on the mind of the reader or listener, which makes Deep Trivedi a pioneer in this field.

To know more about Deep Trivedi,
visit **www.deeptrivedi.com**

DEEP TRIVEDI

DEEP TRIVEDI

Deep Trivedi is a renowned author, speaker and master of psychology. He writes and conducts workshops with an all-pervasive perspective, guiding individuals towards the achievement of their full potential. To date, he has led millions onto the path of success and happiness through his works.

In his voluminous works, Deep Trivedi has extensively explained Nature, its laws, its behaviour, its psychology and the effect it has on human life. No aspect of life and human psychology has been left untouched by him. He states that lack of psychological knowledge and understanding is the sole reason for all the sorrows and failures that pervade human life.

He has authored the bestsellers 'I am The Mind', 'I am Krishna', 'I am Gita', 'Everything is Psychology', '101 All Time Great Stories', 'The Black Book of Soul', '3 Easy Steps To Win At Life' and many more. His bestseller 'I am The Mind' has been published in several national and international languages. He has been awarded the Times Power Men Award 2018 for his immense contribution to society.

His command over the deepest psychologies of life can be gauged by the fact that he holds the record for 'Maximum Workshops on Human Life',

PSYCHOLOGY OF CONFUSION

Table of Contents

A journey from **chaos** to **clarity**

First Edition: 2025

Printed in India

Concept, Illustration and Design:

www.aatmaninnovations.com

Publisher: Aatman Innovations Pvt. Ltd.
Place of Publication: Mumbai

ISBN 978-93-84850-86-9

Psychoanalysis

The Only Solution to Eliminate Problems

Our minds, for centuries, have been confounded by the question—can't life be lived effortlessly, free from troubles? The question is pertinent because in life, troubles are ever ready to knock at one's door, whereas all one wants is peace, joy and progress. This naturally makes one wonder: can't human life be a smooth, joyful ride? So, let me state clearly that humans can certainly live a 'magnificent life', and that too without hindrances or obstacles. There is no constraint as far as their 'capability' is concerned, as every human being is 'naturally capable' of leading a great life.

In fact, Nature has sent humans on earth to live with grace and magnificence, so the very question whether they 'can' lead a great life is erroneous to start with. Ideally, a human being must live a splendid life. So, what's stopping him? Why is his life full of complications? Why is it mired in so many problems? There is only one answer to this—lack of 'psychological knowledge'. It is lack of psychological knowledge that is the root cause of all the problems plaguing human life—no other reason is responsible for this! All the problems a human being is besieged with are 'psychological' in nature and that is precisely why their solutions can also be found only within the scope of psychology. However, due to a dearth of profound psychological knowledge, humans are compelled to suffer on account of their problems. In fact, a glance at human history confirms that no sincere efforts have ever been made to eliminate problems from human life, and even the few, modest efforts that were made through the ages never reached the masses. On the contrary, people have only resorted to playing the 'blame game' under the guise of solving problems, making proclamations such as, 'Anger is a sin!', 'Confusion is wrong!' Alright, they are but what should we do? How do we tackle them? No one has an answer! Lips are sealed and the solutions are drowned in silence. If this weren't enough, motivational speakers step up to profess, 'Get rid of confusion and march forth in life!', 'Make a resolve that from tomorrow onwards, you will not be confused.' But do you really think such silly statements yield positive results? This is precisely why I state that no sincere efforts have ever been made to dispel problems from human life. And this is the very reason why I dissect every subject and psychoanalyse it in depth. Because to eliminate any problem from its root, it is imperative to trace it back to its point of origin—the point from where it began. Simply put, just as it is impossible to ascertain the cause of death without conducting a complete 'post-mortem', it is not possible to ascertain the root cause of a problem without psychoanalysing it in depth. And a complete psychoanalysis implies tracing the problem back to its 'point of origin', examining it in depth and eventually arriving at its 'concluding point'. Believe me, it is only through such deep and consistent effort that problems can truly be resolved and overcome.

So, let us first comprehend what psychoanalysis actually means. Psychoanalysis is the process of identifying a problem in its entirety and arriving at a foolproof solution. If even a single aspect is overlooked in a psychoanalysis, the entire matter becomes psychologically incorrect. But let alone covering all aspects, one is often unable to fathom even the basic aspects of a matter. And yet, those who make tall claims continue to do so and those who want to write tomes on it continue to write! Amusingly, those who are keen on listening to such frivolous talks, continue to listen as well. This is why centuries have elapsed but no 'permanent solution' has been found to eliminate the problems plaguing human life. Humans continue to face the same-old problems they were struggling with since time immemorial. And this is a serious matter indeed! To continue living like this surely does not befit the 'evolved human being' in today's scientifically advanced age. I am certain, you will all agree with the point I have made.

And if you concur with me, let us all come together and determinedly decide that enough is enough! Centuries have passed and yet, we have not been able to find definite solutions to our problems—and this cannot be tolerated anymore! Living in an advanced age with an evolved intelligence, we cannot succumb to baseless and frivolous notions. Today, we can delve into the core of every problem and also look for its solution. In this day and age, we cannot throw up our hands and say, 'If the human being living thousands of years ago was suffering the same ordeals, how can we hope to live differently?' No! We must find solutions to our problems, no matter what! We must live a magnificent life, come what may! And to that end, first and foremost, it is essential to grasp that every problem plaguing human life is psychological in nature. Without an in-depth psychoanalysis, neither can one delve into the root of a problem nor find a solution. In fact, listening to frivolous and non-psychological talk will only increase one's chances of going astray. Therefore, from today onwards, turn a deaf ear to non-psychological drivel. In fact, as a first step, we must rid ourselves of the absurd ideas and notions that have taken root within us. For, what is the point in 'lugging the weight' of ideas that have proved useless in solving our problems, despite believing in and

Wrong teachings lead to wrong actions and wrong actions bring undesirable outcomes

holding on to them for centuries? So, you must first prepare yourself to listen to and imbibe profound, psychological ideas, as it is only then that you will be able to fathom the in-depth psychoanalysis of any matter. On failing to do this, the outdated, baseless talks that you have assimilated over the years will continue to delude you, preventing new and profound thoughts from entering your mind. So, as a primary step, decide that from today onwards, you will listen to and assimilate only profound and psychologically correct notions, while steering clear of frivolous and baseless talks. This decision on your part will secure a firm, first step towards 'finding solutions to your problems'. Indeed, it is one thing to be ignorant, but it is a far serious problem if you fall prey to wrong ideas and notions. So, unless you stop being stubborn about paying heed to baseless talks, you will not find solutions to your problems—even if you keep trying all your life! You need to realise that if your mind has already become a dumping ground for nonsensical ideas, then the fresh ideas and thoughts entering it will be tossed around with the stale, outdated ideas and eventually rendered useless. Any new object in a room will add to its beauty only when the room is spruced up and cleaned of all the mess in it. So, my sole request to you is: since you are an intelligent person, behave accordingly. If you allow yourself to be trapped in baseless notions, your life will slip out of your hands, leaving you tangled up in complications for no reason. Thus, start showing interest in profound and psychologically correct talks. Life is a rare and beautiful opportunity to 'live magnificently', not to be wasted due to ignorance, ego or obstinacy.

At this point, you might interject saying *'Yes, we admit that problems and complications are a big part of our*

PSYCHOLOGY
PROBLEMS

There is only one reason for every problem in life and that is ignorance of psychology

lives! We also agree that despite efforts being made for centuries, we have failed to find concrete solutions to our problems. But kindly explain, why are you emphasising so much on 'psychoanalysis' to achieve this?' Well, that is because without conducting a complete psychoanalysis, it is impossible to find a foolproof and permanent solution to any problem. Nature is a science and so is human life. Psychology and psychoanalysis are also sciences in themselves. And the very definition of 'science' is that everything functions in accordance with 'predetermined laws'. It, therefore, becomes imperative to conduct an in-depth psychoanalysis to both comprehend a problem and find the right solution. For, psychoanalysis is a scientific manner of dissecting 'psychological matters'. And indeed, it makes no sense for the evolved man in today's scientific age to discuss baseless, unscientific ideas. In ancient times, when man's consciousness had not evolved to great heights, it was still alright to profess unscientific and absurd ideas—but not in today's era! So, do not ask me again why it's crucial to conduct an in-depth psychoanalysis of every issue.

The crux of the matter is, one cannot allow this precious life, bestowed upon a human being, to go to waste under the influence of absurd ideas. Introspect your own life and you will realise that it is mired in complications only because of the 'non-psychological' ideas you have imbibed. Hence, I would request, instead of reading and listening to unscientific and non-psychological ideas, live as per 'your own understanding and intelligence'. Believe me, if it weren't for the misguided beliefs and notions leading everyone astray, each person inherently knows 'how to carve a splendid life'. It is the absurd, non-psychological ideas propagated over time that have clouded everyone's understanding; otherwise, no life would be grappling with so many complications.

So, you must live either as per your own understanding and intelligence or listen to only profound and psychologically correct ideas. It is my firm conviction that if you safeguard yourself from falling prey to wrong, unscientific and baseless notions, you will have won half the battle already. For, 'wrong ideas and notions' lead to 'wrong actions' which invariably result in 'undesirable outcomes'. With this statement, I have made a significant point and also given you a compelling hint. So, from now on, never question why you should avoid paying attention to flawed and unscientific ideas and discussions. If you wish, read the above-mentioned statement twice. And since you are intelligent, I trust that mere indications would suffice. I, therefore, request you to start reading and comprehending 'profound psychological truths' as doing so will free you from your problems one by one. Honestly, I have elaborated on this subject only to prepare you to do this.

What is the Root Cause of Confusion?

In our discussion so far, we have understood that without delving into the root cause of a problem i.e. without a complete psychoanalysis, it is impossible to find a solution. This means that since problems have not been analysed in depth psychologically, they have prevailed for centuries. Five thousand years ago, humans were gripped by anger, jealousy, frustration, confusion and more, and even today, modern-day humans are grappling with the same set of problems. But why? Because an in-depth psychoanalysis was never conducted before. It, therefore, becomes imperative to first comprehend what psychology essentially is. Simply put, the core function of psychology is to conduct a thorough post-mortem of every matter. Moreover, its scope extends beyond the human 'mind'. Psychology conducts an in-depth analysis of everything, from objects, people and circumstances to mind, life and Nature. Broadly speaking, this is the essence of psychology and its function too. This in itself can help you gauge the vast scope of psychology. However, let me also clarify that although conducting a post-mortem of the human mind is the primary function of psychology, it is certainly not its limit, as psychology is far more vast and profound.

At present, though, I want you to answer a simple question: how would you define a doctor? I'm sure you would say a doctor is a medical practitioner who diagnoses physical illnesses in human beings. Well, in a similar vein, those who diagnose the 'ills plaguing the human mind' are called psychologists. Now, tell me, what does a doctor do after diagnosing an illness? He uses his expertise to treat the illness. This means that someone who cannot diagnose an illness and is not qualified to treat it can only be called a quack! So, the primary condition is that a doctor or a psychologist, for that matter, should both be qualified and equipped to deal with illnesses i.e. a doctor must be adept at both diagnosing an illness as well as treating it, for only then can he truly be called a 'doctor'. Here, you must also understand that it is not just humans who possess a mind; every visible and invisible entity has a mind of its own. And to comprehend this point in detail, read the book *'Everything is Psychology'* authored by me. For the time being, just grasp the fact that right from objects to circumstances and from human beings to Nature, everything in existence possesses a mind of its own. And to conduct a complete post-mortem of all these entities falls under the purview of psychology. In short, understanding and explaining the 'what, why and how' of everything falls under the purview of psychology.

Setting this aside for a moment, let me ask you: who are those individuals who invariably condemn and name-call when they see someone struggling with illnesses? Who are those who proclaim that anger, lust, jealousy, ego, confusion are sins, and that violence, theft and irreligiousness are crimes? From a psychological perspective, such people are either ignorant about the subject or have limited knowledge about it. They are the ones who have themselves fallen prey to these afflictions. Besides, all they are doing is simply rattling off the names of illnesses, the way an ordinary person would list physical ailments such as migraine, liver cirrhosis etc. Now, the pertinent point is—just by rattling off the names of illnesses, one does not become a doctor. And neither does anyone become a doctor by merely labelling illnesses as bad. Any disease, be it mental or physical, is harmful for sure. I don't think anyone needs to be told that a headache is detrimental to health. Similarly, no one needs to be explained that confusion and jealousy are harmful. Hence, do not be deluded by people who resort to condemnation and name-calling. I have already warned you against paying heed to such absurd, superficial and baseless talks, because they are psychologically incorrect. So, don't ever be ensnared in the trap of those who engage in superficial talks. Honestly, it is these very people propounding such superficial notions that have further corrupted your mind and aggravated your condition. Labelling these ailments as sins does not make them vanish; on the contrary, it only traps you in the guilt of having fallen prey to them. In fact, it would be far better to leave the illness untreated, as it may eventually resolve on its own. Many ailments, whether physical or mental, tend to resolve on their own over time. Thus, unless you fully understand the complete psychoanalysis of 'anger', do not label 'anger' as bad. Once again, I have made a profound point, so do yourself a favour by not getting swayed by superficial and half-baked knowledge—else, you will only be ensnared further. Arrive at every decision only after grasping the matter in its entirety. I am asserting this point emphatically because whether it is human life or the cosmos, both are immensely vast and profound. They cannot be fathomed on the basis of superficial or half-baked knowledge.

Having said that, the central theme of this book is 'confusion' and our ultimate goal is to dispel the ailment called confusion from our lives. However, since it was necessary for you to comprehend the difference between psychological and non-psychological notions, I have addressed this point at the outset of the discussion. From here onwards, we will direct our attention towards comprehending 'confusion'. But first, answer this: What

Confusion is no ordinary ailment...it is an epidemic

are we truly concerned about—confusion or the human being? Take a moment to reflect on this before answering.

I'm sure you'd all agree that we are concerned only about the human being, not confusion itself. We are addressing confusion solely because of its detrimental impact on the human being. Otherwise, humans are our one and only concern. And this principle applies not just to confusion, but to all ailments that affect human life. We are not concerned with the illness itself, but with the person who is afflicted by it; whereas all non-psychological talks label the illness as a sin, focusing exclusively on it and leaving the one grappling with it to 'suffer' alone. But not anymore! We will now discuss only that which is psychologically correct. Our focus will solely be on the 'one afflicted with the illness', and to address that, we must gain a deep understanding of the person who is suffering; in other words, grasp the psychological nature of a human being. This will be our starting point as we begin to delve into the root cause of confusion. For, as important as it is to comprehend the illness, it is equally important to understand the person affected by it. After all, the illness has nothing to lose—the afflicted is the one who suffers.

Well, now that we have determined that it is the human being we are concerned about, I want you to answer a simple question: what is a human being essentially? A human being is a creature with the most evolved consciousness, capable of scaling as many heights of joy and progress as he desires. Although, having this evolved consciousness is not the human being's problem, nor is his ability to make progress. These are, in fact, matters of pride and dignity. So, what's his problem then? I'm sure everyone can list a myriad of problems, and it is clear that humanity is struggling with many. But the question is, what is the 'root cause' of these problems? Has anyone ever reflected on this? If you'd like, take a moment to reflect on it and then respond. It is only when you engage in these small reflections that your psychological understanding will deepen. And this understanding is crucial, as until now, you have only been familiar with the names of these problems or illnesses. No one has ever explored what lies at the root of them. At the most, people, under the guise of motivation, goad you by posing questions such as, 'Why are you always confused? Rise, wake up and move past it! What are you waiting for?' But we rise and wake up every day—yet, does our confusion vanish simply by doing so? Therefore, I will neither label confusion as bad or wrong, nor ask you to simply move past it. Instead, I will conduct an in-depth psychoanalysis of confusion, uncovering all the underlying causes, and then provide insights into how to overcome it. To fully benefit from this, all you need to do is work on sharpening your 'psychological insight'.

Well, setting aside the viewpoints of others, let us come back to our key question—what lies at the root of all human problems? Since you are gripped by problems day in and day out, why have you never paused to reflect on this crucial point? When you wish to eliminate problems from your life, why haven't you pondered the cause? There is only one reason for this: everyone has been taught only to talk about the names of illnesses and label them as sins. This is precisely why I had asked you to reflect on the 'root cause of problems'. I'm sure most of you have already reflected on this and even identified the 'root cause'. But for those who haven't, let me explain. *'Karma'* i.e. deeds lie at the root of all problems plaguing human life. Nature has designed the human being in such a manner that he has to perform *'karma'* from the moment he is born till the time he departs the world. Without performing *karma*, he cannot 'attain' anything in life. Let me make it absolutely clear that for a human being, even resting for a moment is a *karma*, and every breath taken and released is also a *karma*. In short, without performing *karma*, a human being cannot even 'live' for a second. This implies that *'karma'* (deed) is the foundation of human life, and any problem stems only from the 'base' or 'foundation'. So, essentially, deeds are the foundation of a human being's life and this very foundation is the point of origin for all his problems. So, from today onwards, no matter what kind of problem you are faced with or the nature of its complication, take a good look at your 'deeds'. For, it is in your deeds that you will be able to trace the starting point of every problem. I have explained a profound psychological principle to you, and I want you to learn how to effectively apply these deep principles in every area of your life. I promise you, by embracing and imbibing all these profound principles, your life will transcend newer heights of success and happiness. So, if you'd like, make a note of all the principles I am sharing here. Grasp well that the very meaning of a 'principle' is that it is applicable in all situations and spheres of life.

Now, let us move on to our main topic of discussion—confusion, as the sole objective of this book is to rid oneself of all kinds of confusion forever. As stated earlier, *karma* is the 'base' or 'foundation' of all problems affecting human life, and confusion is no exception. But what is confusion after all? Confusion is nothing but grappling with contradictory thoughts; for instance, 'What should I do?' 'What should I avoid doing?' 'Whose advice should I heed?' 'Whom should I trust?' 'Where should I go or where should I avoid going?' 'Which actions will lead to a positive outcome and which ones will bring negative results?' 'Should I choose this place or another?' 'When is the right time to do something, and when should I choose a different course of action?' In short, there are a million confusions that you grapple with on a daily basis, but they all revolve around *karma* alone. Here, you must also grasp that even 'thinking' and 'wishing for something' are 'deeds' in themselves. In other words, even worries pertaining to 'what I must achieve' and 'how to achieve it' are nothing but 'deeds'. This proves that deeds are undeniably the root cause of all kinds of confusion.

A confusion-free person can 'live' more fully and 'achieve' a lot more too

Well, I'm sure you have understood by now that *karma* lies at the heart of all the problems humans face, which is why no 'confusion' exists which does not have *'karma'* at its root. If you notice, with a simple psychoanalysis on our part, we have traced the 'point of origin' of confusion and also learnt that all our confusions are related solely to *'karma'*. This realisation is a great achievement in itself! So, from now on, whenever you find yourself confused, take a moment to check what lies at its root. You'll discover that, at its core, there is always *'karma'*. In my opinion, through a simple conversation that helped us identify the source of confusion, we have already taken a significant step towards sharpening our psychological insight. And truly, my goal is to help everyone continually refine their psychological insight because without it, one cannot live a smooth and effortless life. Centuries have passed in irrelevant discussions, yet to this day, we have not been able to find concrete solutions to our problems. So, to make great strides in life, everyone must realise the importance of enhancing their psychological insight. And it is for this purpose that I am trying to touch upon all aspects of this subject. For, I believe that instead of merely scratching the surface of a topic, it is crucial to dive deep into it. Honestly, in addition to conducting a complete psychoanalysis of confusion, my primary goal is to improve your psychological understanding too. And by delving into the 'root cause of confusion', we have already set ourselves on that path. The direction we have picked is crucial, otherwise you would have still been grappling with pointless statements such as 'confusion is not good' and 'why are you always confused'. But now, we have come to understand that at the root of every confusion lies some form of *'karma'* i.e. deeds. In other words, all our confusions pertain to *'karma'* alone.

Human Confusion
Has No Limit

The great scientist, Albert Einstein had once said, "Two things are infinite: the universe and human stupidity, and I'm not sure about the universe." And today, I say with conviction that while it may be possible for the universe to have a limit, human confusion is limitless. It is quite common to see humans gripped by confusion multiple times a day. After all, is there any subject that doesn't leave them perplexed? Whether it is life's profound questions or the simple choices they face daily, confusion is their constant companion. Questions such as 'Does God exist or not?' and 'Is rebirth a fact or myth?' have confounded the human race for ages. Despite the passage of time, the vast majority still finds itself bewildered by these fundamental questions of life.

While confusion about life's ultimate questions is understandable, it is harder to accept when a person finds himself confused about every little matter. In fact, confusion has become so entrenched in human life that many are left uncertain—even about simple decisions such as, 'what actions to take or what to avoid'. This confusion extends to relationships as well, where individuals frequently grapple with uncertainty. Few can state with absolute clarity whom they truly share a deep bond with and who are merely acquaintances; who is a friend and who is a foe. Such perceptions shift from day to day. It suddenly becomes unbearable to spend even a single moment with your spouse, with whom you once dreamt of spending several lifetimes.

Reflect upon your own life! You will realise it has turned into an unending series of confusions. Is there anyone who has not been confused about 'Which subject to choose in school or college?' or 'Whether they should marry or not?' Is there anyone who has not been confused about matters such as, 'Whom should I choose for a life partner?', 'Which career should I pursue?' or 'Which business should I undertake?' Regardless of the situation, a person inevitably finds himself confused.

This prompts the question: why are so many people constantly struggling with confusion? It might be understandable if only ten to twenty percent of the population was caught in a state of confusion. But when the vast majority is afflicted by it, it becomes a matter of serious concern. After all, confusion is not a figment of one's imagination, floating in the air, or a random force falling from the sky. If that were the case, it might still be understandable. But we have never heard of a phenomenon that the city of New York was caught in a deluge of 1000 tonnes of confusion! In other words, Nature cannot be held responsible for our confusion. Let me also clarify that everything that unfolds in a human being's life is either because of 'Nature' or the 'human being' himself. So, it goes without saying that if anyone is to blame for the affliction called confusion, it is the human being himself. To blame God, destiny or past *karma* reflects a gross misunderstanding of 'psycho-spirituality'. There is only one absolute psychological truth: a human being himself is responsible for all the issues that aren't created

The helpless human being, misled by his flawed beliefs, acts as if 2+2=5, only to be confused by the actual result of 2+2=4

by Nature. Unlike tsunamis or earthquakes, confusion is not something that Nature has created or forced upon us. In short, an individual is solely responsible for the confusion clouding his mind. And only those who acknowledge this truth and take responsibility for it will be able to overcome their problems. For everyone else, each new day will only bring more confusion.

Now that we realise that we ourselves are responsible for the growing confusion in our lives, let us ask ourselves: what is the real reason behind a human being becoming so mired in confusion? There is only one underlying cause—not just of confusion but of all the problems plaguing human life—and that is 'lack of psychological knowledge'. I have given a profound hint here, so remember it forever. Understand once and for all that only an individual who develops a deep 'psychological understanding' will overcome not just confusion but all other problems in his life. This alone highlights the importance of understanding psychology.

To sum up, our psychoanalysis so far has given us a clear insight into three fundamental points. First, *karma* lies at the core of all confusion, which simply means that every confusion is rooted in and arises from *karma.* Second, regardless of the problem one faces, it exists solely because of a lack of psychological knowledge in that area. Third, problems that are not directly caused by Nature are a human being's own creation. In other words, a human being himself is the creator and orchestrator of these problems. Consider this: in just the first few pages of this book, we have uncovered three key points. Ensure that you embed them in your mind, as they will not only help

It is a fundamental principle of psychology that the only way to cure a disease is by eliminating its root cause

you fathom the essence of this book but also guide you towards carving a splendid life for yourself.

Now, let us explore the root cause of confusion by conducting a thorough psychoanalysis, for whether it is confusion or any other problem in life, the only way to overcome it is through an in-depth psychoanalysis. And I am sure you must have already prepared yourself to do this, especially now that you know there is no limit to the confusion plaguing human beings.

Confusion

A Dangerous Disease

Before we begin the complete psychoanalysis of confusion, let us first address any misconceptions you might have about the significance of this book. This is crucial because human nature cannot be trusted at all. Many might say, 'If we're confused, so be it! What difference does it make? Confusion is not an ailment that warrants such deep concern.' If you are thinking on these lines, the very purpose of this book will be undermined—and I will not allow that to happen. So, let me be clear: confusion is no ordinary ailment; it is, in fact, a dangerous disease. So, never dismiss it by saying, 'If we're confused, so be it. How does it matter?' It is vital to clarify how grave confusion is, because only then will everyone take it seriously. After all, it is disastrous to treat cancer as a mere headache, and I don't want confusion to be dismissed in the same way. It is, therefore, essential to explain why eliminating confusion is of utmost importance.

In the context given above, let me first ask you: what is the purpose of human life? Undoubtedly, it is to live to the fullest and reach remarkable heights—indeed, there can be no other purpose. Therefore, grasp well that confusion acts as a hindrance in achieving both these purposes. And if something proves to be an obstacle in achieving the main purpose of life, wouldn't you call it a grave problem?

At this point, you might interject, 'But how can confusion be a hindrance to living life? How does it thwart our progress?' I know that you will not believe me without adequate proof. These questions are natural and bound to cross your mind! Besides, you should never accept anything without being fully convinced of it. So, for now, let's start with a simple question: what is the game of life all about? Without a doubt, this game is all about 'time'. Each person has a limited life span, typically around 80–100 years, and everything a person achieves must also fall within this timeframe. Now, whether you want to live to the fullest or make your mark in this world, what is it that you need to do? Clearly, you need to perform your *karma* i.e. your deeds. And under what circumstances do you fail to perform your *karma*? It is when you are confused about it. So, just think, if you are constantly confused about every aspect of your life, what will happen? You won't be able to perform your tasks, which means you won't be able to shape a great life. Worse still, you will receive far less than you deserve. Therefore, do not underestimate how dangerous this disease called confusion is! In fact, the beauty of accurate and profound psychology is that the proof becomes evident in the explanation itself.

Based on the explanation above, one can surmise that a confusion-free person will be able to perform deeds for approximately 60 years in a total lifespan of 80 years, assuming the remaining 20 years are spent in sleep and rest. In contrast to this, a person who is confused will only manage to perform deeds for about 30 years, as he will spend the other 30 years wading in a sea of confusion, questioning which actions to take and which to avoid. And this will ultimately reduce his 'mileage' of deeds. And I need not explain the simple math that fewer deeds will produce fewer results. So, I hope it is now clear what a loss-making proposition it is to live in a state of confusion. You must have realised that if your life feels incomplete, it is only because of confusion. Any type of confusion instantly puts the brakes on the deed at hand, whereas the fact remains that one must perform *karma* to attain both happiness and progress in life. So, whether you want to live to the fullest or leave your mark on this world, you must triumph over confusion. Ask yourself: what is the point of putting your life on a 'discount sale'? 'I will live only thirty percent and progress only twenty percent. My life is on a discount sale, so I will spend the remaining part of it grappling with confusion. I will while away my life in a confused state of mind, swinging back and forth between 'What should I do?' and 'What should I not do?' I will continue to ruminate over 'Why I should or shouldn't perform a particular task'.' Now, you may have put your life on a discount sale, but I will not allow it—I will steer it in a fruitful direction. And with that intention, we will dive deeper into the psychoanalysis of confusion. All you need to do is stay open-minded and absorb everything that is being shared in all its profundity. I assure you, with this little effort on your part, we will surely gain victory over confusion.

The Fundamental Reason Behind Confusion

It is amply clear that confusion instantly impacts the flow of life, because a confused state of mind directly puts a pause on *karma*. And a 'pause' implies that the amount of time spent taking a pause was wasted needlessly without doing anything. Let me remind you that the entire game of life is dependent on 'time', so a confused person loses out on the opportunity to execute and achieve a great many things that he would have otherwise accomplished. In other words, when a person is free from confusion, he can 'live' more fully and even 'achieve' a great deal more. That is why it is essential to make a concerted effort to eliminate the affliction called confusion. And to do so, the first step is to identify its root cause.

So, let us straightaway dive into the reason behind man's perpetual state of confusion. Where does it all stem from? Why does every person, to varying degrees, fall prey to confusion? Well, the main reason is that most people are unaware that the entire cosmos functions in accordance with set laws. Truth be told, the vast majority is oblivious to the very design of Nature. Many are ignorant about the fact that every particle in the cosmos follows established laws, and this applies to human mind and life as well. And since everything is governed by laws, it operates like the irrefutable mathematical formula: '2 + 2 = 4'. No matter what the brain thinks or the mind imagines, one cannot alter this equation to '2 + 2 = 5'.

In essence, the world operates as an interplay of science, mathematics and psychology. It is scientific because everything is governed by set laws; mathematical because 2 + 2 will always add up to 4; and psychological because the 'mind' continues to take flights of fancy that are beyond the reach of science and mathematics. And this is where psychology undoubtedly comes into play. Well, since we have established that the world is a combination of science, mathematics and psychology, what happens is that on one hand, everything transpires as per set laws, but on the other hand, the human being desires everything as per the flights of his 'mind'. To explain this principle in simpler terms, everything occurs in accordance with fixed laws, but the human being desires outcomes based on his psychological imprudence. This creates a clash between the two, which results in him getting confused. So, if you want to get rid of confusion, grasp clearly that Nature functions on a predetermined set of laws, while the mind too has its own separate laws. *Karma* has its own set of laws and so does life. In fact, every visible and invisible entity has its own distinct laws which are applicable in the strictest sense i.e. they cannot be contravened. And if one wants to live a smooth and effortless life, one will have to abide by these laws. Basically, it is impossible to contravene or violate these laws. At this point, I'd recommend noting down these insights, as they will benefit and guide you in various stages and situations in life.

Well, we have fully grasped the truth that everything in this world is governed and bound by laws. Simultaneously, we have understood that the human being is living in complete ignorance of these laws. But this is just one aspect of the matter. The twist is that humans are not compelled to abide by these laws! In this vast cosmos, the human being is the only creature whom Nature has bestowed with a fully active mind, brain and ego, all of which operate freely in the realm of thought. Here, you must pay attention to my words as I reiterate: these three faculties are completely free to think their own thoughts. And this means they are also free to harbour thoughts that are in contradiction to the laws of Nature. In other words, there is no constraint or restriction on 'thinking' ideas or notions that go against the laws of Nature.

This might prompt you to wonder, 'Well, so what if a human being, in his ignorance about 'Nature's design', harbours thoughts and ideas that go against these laws. What's the harm in that?' Well, the problem is that first, he entertains ideas that contradict the laws of Nature, and then he acts on them. Moreover, once he starts to think, he doesn't stop at just 'thinking'. Unaware of Nature's laws, he starts believing that his faulty reasoning—like thinking '2+2 equals 5'—is correct. Regardless of whether one is truly sensible or not, who doesn't believe themselves to be intelligent? As a result, everyone busies themselves with performing actions that align with their misguided calculations, trying to make 2+2 add up to 5.

Well, this is still understandable, but the biggest twist is that 'laws' do not change just because a human being is misled and acts in accordance with his flawed beliefs. In other words, a human being might perform his deeds as per his calculation (2 + 2 = 5), but the results will always manifest according to Nature's irreversible law (2 + 2 = 4). This is because the 'laws' are not concerned with human thinking. The laws operate continuously, 24/7, of their own accord. And this is where a human being becomes confused and finds himself stuck. With this example, I have hinted towards the biggest predicament of your life. So, if you'd like, read the above explanation multiple times. Do whatever it takes, but ensure that you grasp the profundity of this matter thoroughly. Trust me, you will not come across the opportunity to comprehend such profound mysteries of life so frequently.

If a problem arises from 'ignoring the laws' the only way to find a solution is by 'following the laws'

Considering the significance of this point, let me explain it again in simpler terms. Imagine a scenario wherein a person first thinks of breaking traffic rules (for example, running a red light), and then he also mistakenly believes that he has succeeded in breaking the signal. But in reality, he is not able to break the signal, because the 'signal of Nature's laws' cannot be broken at all. In short, he is first confused about whether he should break the signal or not, and later whether he has broken the signal or not. Simply put, the helpless human being, misled by his own delusional thinking, performs all his tasks thinking '2+2 will add up to 5', but when the actual result of '2+2 adding up to 4' emerges, he is confused. In other words, he is initially confused about whether he should perform the deed or not, then he is uncertain if he actually did it, and once the result appears, he is confused about what really happened and how. The example I have given here reflects everyone's experiences in life on a daily basis. Every outcome puzzles an individual as to how such an eventuality came to pass! 'This is certainly not the outcome I had wanted and definitely not something I had even thought would happen.' Frustrated thus, he wonders why his actions did not align with his thinking and intentions. However, you must realise that any *karma* (action) stemming from confusion will inevitably lead to confusing results. This is why, oftentimes, what we expect doesn't match what actually happens. Can anyone say with certainty that everything they thought would occur has happened? Probably not. But imagine how extraordinary life would be if your thoughts materialised exactly as you imagined. Unfortunately, as long as confusion reigns supreme, the reality will never align with what we envision. And the root cause of all human confusion is simple:

To carve a spectacular life, you must accomplish maximum number of deeds—and that can only happen when you make decisions swiftly

'ignorance of Nature's laws'. Worse still, humans have the freedom to think contrary to these laws and act based on those misguided thoughts. Here, I have revealed a profound truth to you which encompasses all the reasons that give rise to confusion.

Well, we have identified the root cause of confusion, the very source from which all confusion arises. And the best part is, we have done this effortlessly through a simple psychoanalysis. We have learnt that ignorance of Nature's laws and the tendency to think we can contravene them are the primary reasons for all confusion. This implies that once a person becomes aware of these laws and stops trying to go against them, confusion can be eliminated from his life. Bear in mind that without doing this, one cannot get rid of confusion, even if one tries to move heaven and earth! I encourage you to read this point over and over until you fully understand both the causes of confusion and the way to overcome it. For, only then can you experience true relief from confusion. Here, let me point out, by delving into profound psycho-spirituality and discussing matters from a scientific and psychological perspective, we have not only identified the root cause of confusion, but have also arrived at the solution. In any case, it is a fundamental principle of psychology that the only way to cure an ailment is by eliminating its root cause. For example, if a headache is caused by acidity, treating the acidity is the only effective solution. These are significant psychological truths, so I urge you to apply them wisely at every stage of your life.

Moving ahead with our discussion, it is truly shocking that for centuries, humanity has remained oblivious to these laws. Only a handful of people understand that everything in this world operates according to its own laws. The point worth grasping is that when Nature has already established laws for everything, there is no room for additional laws to be created. Nature's laws cannot be changed, nor will they ever alter. But despite this, humans, driven by their brain and ego, keep creating their own laws. Regrettably, these are what they label as religion, society and even knowledge! However, if we truly wish to free humanity from the problems it has been facing for centuries, we must speak plainly and directly. Indeed, the time has come to find a permanent solution to every problem.

The crux of the matter is that everything in existence is governed by laws. Unfortunately, misguided individuals, for centuries, have been creating their own laws. And if this were not enough, the intelligent among us have also started inventing new laws for themselves. And it is this very act of creating new laws that has ruined everyone's lives. For, Nature is not 'dealing' with everyone based on man-made laws; it is dealing with everyone as per its own, established laws. Yet, in their ignorance, humans continue to act as per their self-made laws. This is why things never unfold as they expect, and only lead to greater confusion about which actions to take and which to avoid.

Let me explain this point using a simple example. No matter what game you're playing, there are always rules that must be followed, right? Every game has its own set of rules, and it is impossible to play without them, because in the absence of rules, you would be clueless about how to play the game! Moreover, without rules, how will you determine the winner or loser? This is precisely the point I'm trying to drive home that life too follows certain laws. And since these laws are already established in the game of life, some people end up 'losing' while some emerge as 'winners'. Have you grasped the point I'm making? If you haven't, let me explain it with an everyday example. Imagine you're playing a game of carrom. A fundamental rule of carrom is that you cannot win without claiming the queen! So, let's say someone decides to play carrom but doesn't know the rules. He comes up with his own rule that whoever claims the queen will lose the game. What do you think will happen in this scenario? Here, you also need to understand that the person who thinks that whoever claims the queen will lose, is free to think so and can choose not to take the queen if he wishes. However, will he actually win the game?

No, because the official rules of carrom still apply, and the umpire will declare him the loser.

This is exactly how the game of life works as well. From the mind and Nature to *karma* and life, everything operates according to its own set of laws. However, since the vast majority is unaware of these laws, they have created their own rules for everything. And if that weren't enough, others, under the guise of offering knowledge, have imposed additional laws on them. But none of these are the 'true, established laws' of life. Yet, people place great importance on these made-up laws and approach life believing them to be the 'laws of life'. This is precisely why, day after day, the umpire called Nature declares the human being a loser in the game of life!

Essentially, man is sabotaging his own life by trying to impose upon himself the laws he has created. He is playing the game of life according to a 'few man-made rules', whereas life follows a different set of laws designed by Nature. Consequently, he remains confused and fails to win the game of life. I hope you have grasped the point I'm trying to convey. This world operates on 'two types of laws'—those created by Nature and those created by humans. While everything is unfolding as per Nature's laws, humans continue to act based on their own rules. As a result, they are repeatedly checkmated in the game of life. I trust that this simple and direct point is now clear to you. If yes, then from today onwards, do not be 'confused' about which laws to follow. Etch it in your mind that you must never follow a single man-made law, and never disregard any law established by Nature. Unfortunately, even to do this, one must first understand the laws of Nature! But the situation has become so

Those who try to impose their will on life always end up straying from their path

dire that if you were to list a hundred laws, you'd find that most of them are man-made.

By now, you must have realised that without fully understanding the matter at hand, no problem can truly be solved. And since every entity in existence operates according to its own laws, resolving the problems of human life is impossible without knowing these laws. If a problem arises from 'ignoring the laws,' the only way to find a solution is by 'following the laws'. And we can only follow laws once we learn about them. As this book is focused solely on 'confusion', we will now delve deeper into the causes behind confusion, one by one, and explore the laws related to them. I will do my best to help you overcome all your confusion by the time you finish this book, ensuring you live 'a confusion-free life'. But to achieve that, you must first let go of the misconception that life will unfold according to the laws you have created. Life will never heed the laws you have set nor follow them. If you want to succeed in the game of life, you must fully abide by the laws of Nature. Otherwise, you will continue to be confused even in the smallest matters. In this bazaar of life, you will always be put on a 'discount sale'. But I'm certain this isn't the way you want to live. If my faith in you is justified, I'm sure you will approach everything in this book with utmost sincerity and understanding.

Do only good

The Biggest Root Cause of Confusion

In our discussion so far, we have come to understand that by creating his own laws, man has trapped himself. The creators of these laws have long since departed the world, but unfortunately, the modern-day man continues to suffer the repercussions of believing in and adhering to these laws every day. It is regrettable that even in today's advanced age, people still give weight to such baseless laws. This is precisely why I must emphasise once again that knowledge imparted without true understanding has cost humanity dearly. Instead of placing unnecessary importance on such unfounded teachings, it would be far better for people to acquire knowledge based on their own life experiences. I'm not making this statement without reason. I say this because Nature and its secrets are incredibly profound, and the reins of human life lie in the hands of those very secrets, which can also be referred to as laws. Therefore, if you truly wish to understand life and its workings, you must first comprehend the 'design of Nature' and 'follow' its laws. There is no other way! The point is, human life is an ongoing series of *karma* (actions), but how many truly understand the complexity of *karma*? Why don't you realise that countless laws are applicable to even those *karmas* which appear the simplest! This is why Krishna explains in the Bhagavad Gita that the nature of *karma* and its pace (i.e. the way *karma* works) are both extremely profound. He goes on to say that even the most prudent minds fail to comprehend the 'difference between *karmas*'. And this statement made by Krishna is self-evident. We all know that human life revolves around *karma*, and we even perform countless *karmas* every day. But how many understand the true meaning of *karma*? This is exactly why I address every topic with a profound and psychologically correct approach. I neither engage in fanning the ego and offering false assurances, nor do I intend to garner praise by writing what you wish to read. My sole intention is to empower you to scale the pinnacle of success, and that is possible only when you read and grasp profound 'psycho-spiritual' matters. In fact, I never write or speak on any matter that is not anchored in profound psycho-spirituality.

Ideally, no one should speak on any matter without a deep and thorough understanding of the subject; only those with a profound grasp of psychology should speak on such topics. Unfortunately, human history stands testament to the fact that this hasn't always been the case. People have often rambled on matters they believed to be right, without giving it proper thought. For instance: 'Don't lie', 'Control your anger', 'Violence is a sin', 'Stealing is wrong', 'This is the best time to wake up and this is the ideal time to eat', 'Eat this food and avoid that', and so on. Essentially, you have been given an endless list of 'what you should do' and 'what you should avoid', leaving you clueless and floundering in a maze! Now, while most people consider these lists of dos and don'ts to be helpful and harmless, it raises an important question: why did Krishna not preach any of these ideas in the Bhagavad Gita, the ultimate scripture of wisdom? Forget the fact that he did not mention them—an even more significant point is that Krishna himself had spoken lies, committed theft, shown anger and even engaged in violence. This is a powerful clue I'm offering you. Understand well that Krishna is the master of psychology, having a firm grasp of the secrets of Nature. Therefore, he would never advocate baseless ideas like 'which actions you should perform' or 'which actions you should avoid.' Comprehend clearly that a supremely intelligent being like Krishna will neither speak on non-psychological matters, nor be constrained in the limitations of such non-psychological talks. And why do you think that is? Well, that is exactly what you need to understand, and precisely what I am trying to explain.

Honestly, I am left speechless on seeing the sorry state of humanity, mired in confusion due to the endless lists of 'what actions to perform' and 'what to avoid.' And since human life revolves around *karma* (action), these teachings are inherently tied to the actions one must perform or refrain from. The only fault of the human being is that he has given undue importance to such teachings without properly evaluating them. Even worse, he has accepted them without understanding that all such teachings contradict the laws of Nature. As a result, every person is caught in a tussle, torn between such 'illogical teachings' and the 'laws of Nature,' and it is this ongoing struggle that keeps hurling them into a state of confusion.

Surprisingly, the lists of 'what to do or not do', 'what is good or bad', 'what is virtuous or sinful' to even simple matters such as 'what to eat or abstain from' are so lengthy that if compiled into books, they would fill an entire town! This also implies, the instructions are so elaborate that it is nearly impossible to remember them all. Yet, people unquestioningly accept and adopt these lists, tailoring them to fit their caste, religion, society and traditions. If someone follows Hinduism, they adopt the list of Hindu teachings; if they follow Islam, they embrace the list of Islamic practices. This might seem fine, but

In life, every gain carries the shadow of loss, and every loss makes room for gain

ironically, all such lists contradict one another. This is because what is prescribed in one religion is prohibited in another. What one religion or tradition deems virtuous is condemned by another. What is praised by one is criticised by another. This contradiction has only amplified the confusion about 'what one must do or not do.' Just think about how helpless and lost a person must feel in such a situation. To sum it up, those who promoted these teachings had nothing to lose, while the common man has been left bewildered and confused for no reason.

Well, the ones who doled out these lists did so out of naivety, but is it really necessary to place so much importance on them? Certainly not! Yet, the human 'ego' has attached great significance to these lists, simply because the lists of 'which actions one must perform or avoid' carry great importance in the world. Whether in religion or society, following such lists is seen as a mark of 'virtue', while ignoring them often leads to one being labelled a 'sinner'. And needless to say, those seen as virtuous are respected, while those deemed sinful are subjected to criticism and scorn. For example, hailing from a Hindu family, if you do not abide by the mores of Hinduism, you will face a barrage of insults from your family and community. Similarly, if you don't adhere to societal rules, you will be criticised and condemned by society. Even your family members, with their rigid beliefs and ideologies, will judge you for not conforming to these principles. And this is a truth we are all familiar with! Thus, in a bid to gain respect, a person's ego ensures that he complies with such lists and principles. Truth be told, the 'subconscious desire' to appear good and virtuous blinds one. Here, I have revealed a profound truth about your inner system. Comprehend clearly that it is the ego that fuels the 'desire to be seen as virtuous', which in turn makes these lists seem important. Simply put, the more importance a person places on these lists, the more 'egoistic' he is. I have provided you a compelling hint, and I believe there is no need to elaborate further.

In essence, the human ego is a complicated instrument. It has no qualms about being depraved or immoral, but it does not want to be seen as wicked. This is yet another significant clue I'm offering you. While this point may seem simple, it is essential that you grasp it thoroughly. These matters pertain to your inner self, so understanding them shouldn't be difficult. What you need to realise is that the ego has no interest in being virtuous—it is, however, deeply concerned with being perceived as virtuous. And how can one be perceived as 'virtuous'? The answer is simple: by unquestioningly following the lists of 'what to do and what not to do' prescribed by religion, society, family and traditions. This is precisely why the vast majority is reeling under the pressure of these lists that dictate which actions should be performed or avoided. Whether willingly or unwillingly, people are compelled to adhere to them, especially when they are part of a group or community. And this is an undeniable truth! Even you, to some degree, must feel the pressure of such lists and teachings. I hope you have now understood the principle that the more one is enslaved by such lists, the more egoistic one is.

While the facts stated above are clear, you might still wonder, 'What's wrong with people handing out lists of what to do and what not to do?' After all, they only encourage us to do good and avoid the bad. With a few exceptions, no one urges us to commit immoral or criminal acts. No one tells us to steal or engage in violence. They simply advise us to speak the truth and avoid hurting others' sentiments. Your point is valid but consider this: those who advocate such ideas and those who follow them are both mistaken. I'm sure this statement will shock you, and you might respond with, "What's wrong with advising someone to perform good deeds or following noble advice?" Well, there must be something wrong, otherwise such teachings would have produced the desired results. You need to realise that despite centuries of imparting such teachings, vices still persist. And the irony is, in the name of freeing people from these vices, an affliction called 'confusion' has taken over. That is why I'm stressing that, no matter how noble these teachings may seem, they are psychologically flawed, as they contradict the laws of Nature; and how can anything that goes against Nature's laws ever be right?

I'm sure you would exclaim, 'What are you saying? How can such righteous teachings go against the laws of Nature?' Well, let me explain right away. In fact, I have provided a detailed background only to help you understand how dangerous these 'so-called righteous teachings' are. So, to grasp this matter in depth, all you need to do is look at Nature. When you wake up in the morning, take some time to observe the cosmos in its entirety. In fact, I would suggest, spend a whole day observing and making notes of everything you notice. After all, if you can dedicate ten to twenty years of your life to acquire an educational qualification, what's the harm in spending just one day to understand Nature? So, just for today, refrain from reading anything further in this book. Instead, take the time to see if something significant strikes you while you observe the world around you. This exercise is vital because it will enhance your 'observation power', and this improved power will sharpen your intelligence and expand your understanding. So, devote at least one whole day to strengthening this power by keenly observing the workings of the cosmos. You'll be amazed at how far this 'self-discovery through observation' can take you.

Well, I trust you must have made some observations and also noted down relevant points. Let me now share a few insights from my side. During your observation, you must have certainly noticed the sun. So, let me ask you: what *karma* does

Those who fear paying the price or try to gain something without paying the price are forever confused

the sun perform? The sun provides light, energy and vitamin D—undoubtedly, these are all beneficial deeds. But what you also need to consider is whether the sun is doing only this. In the summer, doesn't the sun scorch you with its severe heat? Doesn't it cause water to evaporate, drying up ponds and lakes? Can these actions be considered good deeds?

Now, let's turn to the rivers. You've likely observed a river as well, so tell me: what *karma* do the rivers perform? Clearly, they flow, and their flowing water provides great solace to our heart and mind. They even quench our thirst and supply water for agriculture. Unquestionably, this is a significant and positive *karma*—the rivers are, in fact, our lifeline. Without them, we would perish. But take a moment to reflect: are the rivers engaged only in good deeds? Have you not witnessed the devastation caused by a river during a storm or flood? Do you have any idea how many lives floods have claimed? How many villages have been swept away by ferocious currents? Tell me, can we truly call these 'good deeds' performed by the rivers?

Alright! Let's move on from the sun and the rivers and turn our attention to the winds. Undoubtedly, the wind brings in fresh air and oxygen, without which our very survival would be impossible. Additionally, the cool breeze has a soothing effect on our nervous system, which calms us and alleviates our worries. Yet, these aren't the only actions the wind engages in. At times, it transforms into a fierce storm or hurricane, ravaging entire towns and settlements. The same is true of the sea, which, no doubt, offers great joy when we sit by the shore and admire the frothy waves and serene beauty. The sea also serves as a vital route for transporting goods between countries. However, the sea also births life-threatening tsunamis, doesn't it?

Now, based on these observations, what conclusions can you draw? Surely, you must have realised that in Nature, no entity performs only 'good deeds'. Everything in Nature invariably performs some bad deeds as well. So, tell me, if floods cause destruction, should we abandon the rivers? If the sun scorches us with its heat, should we stop seeking its light? Should we stop venturing to the seashore knowing the fact that storms erupt in the sea? Of course not! Why? Because without the rivers, how would we quench our thirst or grow our crops? Without the sun, where would we obtain light and vitamin D? So, what is the solution? There is only one solution: if you want to quench your thirst, you must accept the floods. If you need sunlight to sustain life, you must endure the heat. If you want oxygen from the air, you must brave hurricanes and storms. And this is precisely what we have been doing since the beginning of time. The truth is, we have no choice; we are bound to do so. Why? Because this is the design of Nature. And as mentioned earlier, it is simply not possible to defy Nature's design or its laws. We cannot 'debate' these laws, nor can we 'analyse' their good or bad effects. The laws of Nature simply exist, and we have no power to change them. Willingly or unwillingly, we are bound to live within the boundaries set by these laws. So, if you want to excel in the game of life, you must accept the 'limitations set by the laws of Nature', just as you must follow the rules of cricket when playing a game of cricket. Comprehend clearly that Nature is neither good nor bad; it is a 'complete balance' of both. I hope this simple point is now clear to you.

Alright! Tell me, what have you observed in the workings of the sun, wind, rivers and sea? If you haven't drawn any conclusion, let me explain. The conclusion is simple: anyone who is doing good deeds is invariably a medium for bad deeds as well. Why? Because Nature has not given any individual the power to perform only good deeds. Nature maintains a delicate balance of both good and bad. For example, the Earth sustains our life with its unerring gravity, but it also wreaks havoc through earthquakes. No entity in the universe is dedicated solely to "good" or "beneficial" actions. This is because Nature inherently balances the good and the bad, and this is precisely why every entity will end up performing both good and bad deeds.

Now, you might argue, 'This applies to insentient objects; how is it relevant to us? We are human beings after all—an intelligent and evolved species that must ensure only good.' Well, this reflects nothing but your ignorance about psychology. Yes, you are human, but you are not from another universe. There is only one Nature governing both the sun as well as our lives. And the laws of Nature, by their very definition, mean that they apply to both equally. So, forget the notion that human beings can do only good; the human being cannot refrain from committing wrong even momentarily, because this is the 'eternal, immutable design of Nature'. And since I discuss only profound psycho-spirituality, I always strive to uphold the highest standard in discussing such matters, because this alone is the truth and solutions can emerge only from the truth.

Understand clearly that no deed performed by the human being will yield only positive results; no matter what action he takes, some negative consequence will inevitably follow. For, this is the 'eternal, irrevocable design of Nature'. Of course, a human being, oblivious to this truth, may well preach about 'doing only good'; he may even believe he is 'doing only good' but that is not the reality. Because the fact remains that even the simple act of breathing results in the death of millions of bacteria. So, should we stop breathing to prevent this? In that case, we would all perish. Ironically, those who preach the idea of doing only good are also breathing, aren't they? They too are committing the bad deed of killing bacteria, aren't they? This is a profound truth that you must grasp in its complete depth. Trust me, you will not come across the opportunity to learn and grasp such profound matters easily.

A human being, by nature, is 'greedy'. He wants everything without giving anything in return

The reality is, no action produces purely positive outcomes. In other words, a deed that is devoid of a bad outcome simply does not exist. Thus, teachings that encourage one to perform 'only good deeds' are misleading, because as soon as you perform an action, some bad outcome will inevitably result from it. For example, focusing on your happiness will cause pain to your loved ones. Trying to protect them from sorrow might require sacrifices on your part. If you devote time to your career, you might end up neglecting family duties. Let's say you have to rush to another city to execute important official work, while your father at home is ailing. In such a scenario, you will end up committing the bad deed of leaving your father unattended. On the other hand, if you stay back to tend to your father, your important work will suffer. Similarly, consuming a strong medicine can harm your liver or kidneys, but if you don't take that medication, your illness will remain untreated. This implies, no matter what action you perform, some wrong will invariably take place. And if some bad will inevitably occur in performing any deed, why have people continued to preach the idea of "doing only good deeds"? It is because they had no inkling about the 'laws of Nature'. Indeed, Krishna did not make an unfounded statement when he said, "O Arjuna, the pace of *karma* is incredibly profound and that is why, even the wisest fail to fathom it."

Well, so be it! Presently, comprehend well that *karma*, by its very nature, is flawed. So, whether *karma* is performed by inanimate objects or human beings, some form of 'bad' will always occur as a by-product—it is simply not possible to perform a deed that is purely good. This is the very 'arrangement' that Nature has put in place for *karma*. Now, this being the case, tell me, what

From the moment he is born till he breathes his last, a human being keeps playing the game of 'gain and loss'

is the ultimate outcome of propagating the idea that 'one must do only good'? It has only resulted in man finding himself mired in confusion, to the point that he has lost the ability to act altogether. While it has been drilled into his head that he must avoid wrongdoing, Nature's design does not allow him to perform only good. That is why whenever he thinks about taking any action, his focus inevitably shifts to the potential negative outcomes, making him wonder whether he should perform the deed or not. He begins to deliberate, 'If I do this, this aspect will get impacted, and if I do that, that aspect will be affected.' And this is how the poor human being gets caught in a dilemma. The moment he begins a task, something always goes wrong elsewhere, and then, sighting the adverse outcome, he instantly puts the *karma* on 'hold'. Indeed, the pressure of misguided teachings causes him to become paralysed, unable to act unless absolutely necessary. And even when he summons the courage to take action, he regrets the consequences, lamenting, 'How did I make this mistake?' In short, humans are caught in a vicious cycle—they lament when they perform a deed and regret when they avoid it. If they perform a certain action, the 'guilt of perpetrating a wrong' gnaws at them; and if they avoid the deed fearing the wrong, they are gripped by the 'remorse resulting from their inability to accomplish deeds'. All of this stems from the false teaching that 'one must do only good'. This belief has overwhelmed the human mind to such an extent that people have become weak from within. They are unable to engage in wrongdoing, and without committing some degree of wrong, nothing good can be accomplished. Honestly, caught in this dilemma, they end up spending the majority of their time debating whether to act or refrain from taking action, ultimately failing to accomplish anything of real significance. Since these are all matters related to your own life, with a little bit of reflection, the truth will become apparent to you.

I'm sure all of this would prompt you to ask: is there a solution to this dilemma? Rest assured, there is, and it is actually quite simple.

However, for now, I'm glad that you have fathomed a profound truth about the 'design of Nature'. As for the confusion over 'good and bad outcomes,' you must understand that in Nature's grand scheme of things, there exists a solution for every problem—this is the very specialty of Nature. So, what's the solution, you ask? The answer is: follow the laws of Nature. When it is not possible to perform an action that will only lead to a positive outcome, stop paying heed to teachings that incapacitate you with concepts like 'do only good.' Do not let such teachings confound you. Drill it in your head that a 'bad outcome' is an inevitable part of any action you take, so even if you perform a good deed, some bad will inevitably follow. Hence, first and foremost, rid yourself of the fear that you're committing a bad deed. Let go of the fear and guilt of potential wrongdoing. Erase from your mind all the lists that compel you to do only good. For example, 'visiting a place of worship' is noble, but not at the cost of your ailing father. And any 'good deed' that is once proven wrong can certainly be proven wrong a thousand times over. So, why give importance to lists and principles that insist on doing only good? If you want to free yourself from the confusion of which actions to take or avoid, begin by discarding the notion that you must 'do only good'. Make this mental shift today, and as we progress, I will share the next steps with you. For now, continue to grasp the points I am sharing.

Well, the first step is to clear your mind of all beliefs that bind you to the idea of 'doing only good' and 'fearing the bad'. Once you've done that, take it a step further by recognising that, as a human being, your intent is not to engage in wrong or immoral acts deliberately. If you harbour any such intention, understand clearly that as a human being, you should not wish to commit vile deeds. If you intentionally engage in a vile deed, you do not deserve to be called a 'human being'. So, as a second step, make a firm resolve to maintain your humaneness. In short, you must not commit any vile deed deliberately.

You are well aware that Nature has endowed humans with intelligence—the kind that no other creature in the cosmos possesses. Now, grasp well that in Nature, nothing exists 'without a reason'. Whether it is an atom or the minutest bacteria, there is a clear purpose behind their existence. So, there must be a definite purpose behind the heightened sense of human intelligence too. And verily, there is! This makes one wonder: why is humanity blessed with such remarkable intelligence? Take a moment to reflect on this, or if you prefer, I will share the answer with you. The reason humans are gifted with intelligence is to enable them to make sensible decisions. And what decisions could these be? Simply put, humans are meant to decide which actions to take and when to take them. This means that every human being is naturally capable of determining when to act and when to refrain from action. For this, he requires no external guidance or reassurance. Unfortunately, teachings that urge humans to 'do only good' have dulled this intelligence. People become so consumed by misguided beliefs that they have lost the ability to determine which actions to take or avoid. This is precisely why I shared the principle of *karma* with you which states that every action inherently carries some negative consequence. Understanding this, you should neither fear the inevitable bad that may accompany any deed nor stubbornly insist on performing only good actions. Your only true goal should be to build a magnificent life based on the strength of your *'karmas'*. However, the predicament is, you will be able to perform a deed only when you decide to act on it. If you spend your life in a perpetual state of indecision and confusion, your life will ultimately amount to nothing. And this is the story of most human lives.

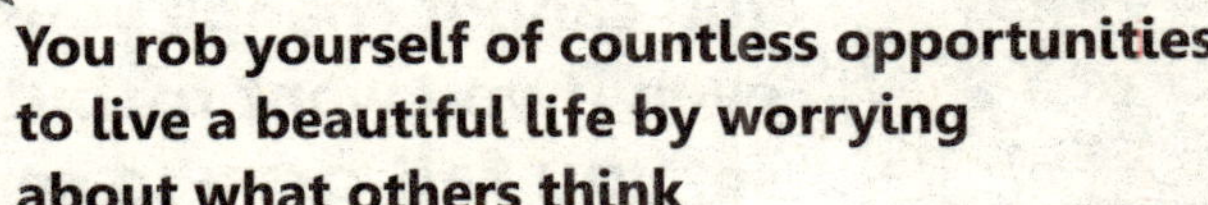

Why not realise that to carve a splendid life, you must accomplish a great number of deeds—and this can only happen if you learn to make decisions swiftly! And you will be able to make quick decisions only when you free yourself from the confusion surrounding *karma.*

In essence, you can make swift decisions only when you accept that every action inevitably involves some negative consequence. And since every deed carries both good and bad outcomes, continue to engage in actions that produce a 'greater good and lesser bad' without being confused. And it is precisely to assess this ratio of good and bad in a deed that humans have been endowed with intelligence—this is the very purpose behind it. Really, I cannot explain this more clearly. Once you grasp this simple psycho-spiritual principle, all your confusion will dissolve on its own. Therefore, I encourage you to erase from your mind all the rigid 'lists' regarding what is 'good' or 'bad'. Do not view any action as permanently good or bad. Instead, focus on performing the deeds that yield more good than bad, and avoid those that result in more bad than good. With this simple, straightforward approach, there will be no room for confusion. Of course, you must not intentionally engage in bad actions. And in the solution I'm proposing, you are indeed not committing any wrong intentionally. Any bad outcome that you are causing inadvertently is simply because of Nature maintaining a 'balance between good and bad'. I trust that you have grasped the profound truth that you are indeed performing good deeds, and the bad is merely a fallout of the inevitable 'bad hidden in every action,' as part of the complex design of *karma.*

Now, let me elaborate this point with the example of Krishna and the exceptional scripture, Bhagavad Gita. As

You cannot change your inner system even if you want to, but in trying to do so, you fall prey to confusion

you know, the Gita commenced when Arjuna refused to fight the Mahabharata war. Why did he refuse? Because he believed it was wrong to kill his brothers, teachers and relatives. He also thought that engaging in such grave violence for a mere kingdom was unwise. To support his argument, he even cited religious texts and scriptures, which condemned such acts, labelling them as sins. You too might find yourself agreeing with Arjuna, and perhaps even sympathising with his predicament. However, this raises an important question: why did Krishna disagree with Arjuna? Was Krishna not a noble man? Did he want Arjuna to commit a wrong? Certainly not! After all, it is hard to find a consciousness as pure as Krishna's. So, why did he encourage Arjuna to commit such gruesome violence? This is the very secret I have been trying to throw light on.

So, pay attention to the essence of what Krishna said to Arjuna. He said, 'What the scriptures term as sin has no relevance to this war. I am standing here next to you, so don't refer to what the scriptures exalt.' The message is simple: no scripture in the world is wiser than Krishna himself. Well, Krishna further explained to Arjuna that all deeds are inherently flawed, having some degree of wrong in them—no deed is entirely free of it. Given this, one cannot avoid performing necessary actions out of fear of the wrong that might follow. So, what are these actions that are worth performing? They are the ones that entail a greater amount of good and lesser amount of bad. For Arjuna, fighting the Mahabharata war was one such action wherein looking at the circumstances, it was far more beneficial for him to fight the war. The war had become inevitable, and whether Krishna and Arjuna participated in it or not, it had to be fought. In other words, the violence and bloodshed could not be avoided. And when violence is unavoidable, the only option is to find some 'greater good' in it. Krishna had already seen the greater good in this inevitable war. As for Arjuna, in his ignorance, he sought to avoid the sin of killing his teachers and relatives, but he failed to see that if he fled the battlefield out of fear of committing this wrong, his entire army would be wiped out. Arjuna was the only expert archer on his side, and his absence would have led to the destruction of his entire army. Given the circumstances, the death of the warriors belonging to one of the two armies was already certain. So, when it was inevitable that one army would be eliminated, the army that would perpetuate atrocities upon winning the war had to be destroyed. That army belonged to the Kauravas—the 'enemy' Arjuna was fighting against. Indeed, had Duryodhana's army won, it would have unleashed even greater violence, leading to more wars in the future. In other words, the conflict that could be resolved by the death of ten thousand men today would have certainly claimed the lives of millions in the future.

In life, understand that it's not always a choice between two good deeds, nor is it necessarily between a good and a bad deed. Life functions in accordance with its own grand *leela*, and in this game of life, one is also confronted with situations where one must choose between two bad deeds. This was precisely the situation in the Mahabharata war, and this is why some people wrongly assume that Krishna was advocating for war. The truth is, Krishna wasn't promoting war or the killing of relatives. Being cognisant of the ultimate secret of life, he was guiding Arjuna to choose the lesser evil. In those circumstances, fighting the Mahabharata war was certainly the lesser of two evils. But of course, it has never been easy to grasp such profound truths and secrets, has it? Hence, the majority of people end up making absurd assumptions and interpretations about Krishna and the Bhagavad Gita in any way they deem fit.

Well, at present, the main question is: when Krishna was absolutely clear about 'what ought to be done', why was Arjuna mired in confusion? It was because he was reeling under the pressure of the teachings that propel one to 'do only good'. And since Krishna was well-versed with the secrets of both life and Nature, he was free from all such nonsensical notions. Moreover, since he did not nurse any such fallacies, he could easily engage in all kinds of deeds, be it cheating, deceiving, theft, lies or killing. Krishna was never confused about any kind of *'karma'*. The thought 'which actions I must perform' or 'which actions I must refrain from' never even crossed his mind. You too must learn to live like Krishna—in a seamless 'flow', free from confusion. So, from this moment onwards, do not be confused about the deeds you have to perform. Ideally, after our discussion, there should be no reason for you to remain confused about 'good and bad deeds'. All you need to do is grasp it well and implement it in your life without delay.

Well, since the point I have made is novel and profound and might even unsettle you—perhaps because you are not accustomed to reading such profound discussions of psycho-spirituality—let me summarise all that we have discussed so far. The key premise of our discussion is that human life is bound by several laws of Nature, and one such law states that every *karma* (action), regardless of who performs it, will contain some inherent flaw. Therefore, fearing the bad outcome, neither can the *karma* be avoided nor can one continue to live in a state of confusion. Life is shaped by actions, not confusion. Understand that every *karma* involves a mix of good and bad, so continue to perform actions that lean more towards good than bad. There is no need to put a deed on hold or be confused about it. Similarly, if you ever encounter a situation in life where you have to choose between 'two bad deeds', then without clouding your mind with confusion, choose the deed that will result in a 'lesser bad outcome'. For example, if kidnappers are trying to abduct a child, you must take action to stop them, even if it involves violence. To claim that violence is wrong in such a scenario would be downright foolish.

Realise this—no one can understand your life, your actions or your happiness better than you do

But yes, your intent must always be pure while performing all kinds of *karma.* Never intentionally commit a bad deed, no matter what the circumstances are. Other than this, you are well aware that you cannot alter the 'design of Nature'. Let others waste their energy in trying to do so, but you must respect the design of Nature under all circumstances without any confusion. In the example given above, remember that you're not thrashing the goons out of malice, but to protect the child. The violence is merely a 'consequence resulting from the complex nature of *karma*'. Those who focus on 'idealistic notions of non-violence' would take no action to stop the kidnappers. Even Arjuna saw the act of killing Duryodhana as a sin, but you must not be like Arjuna. The game of life is such that sometimes, you just cannot save a victim without confronting the wrongdoers. Therefore, don't get caught up in rigid ideas of 'this action is good' and 'that action is bad'. You never know what deed you might have to perform in this game called life. Therefore, always be prepared to perform the best possible deed. For, no one can 'do' anything except 'choose the best possible deed' from all the available options. This is the very design of Nature. So, respect this design and free yourself from all confusion arising from the prescribed lists of 'good' and 'bad'. Profound truths such as this are seldom discussed, so take this opportunity to clear any lingering doubts about 'good-bad' deeds and move forward without confusion.

Practical Application

Alright! Let me provide you with a practical approach to help you get started. In the chart below, list ten most significant deeds you're currently uncertain about. Basically, you need to write down the ten tasks you've put on 'hold' because of your confusion regarding their potential outcomes—whether good or bad. In the adjacent column, estimate the percentage of positive and negative results you expect from each of those deeds. Once you've done that, focus on carrying out the actions that have a higher percentage of a positive outcome, without being confused. With this single exercise, you'll notice a significant increase in the pace of your deeds. And needless to say, the more actions you take, the more remarkable your life will become.

No.	Deed	% of Good	% of Bad	Decide whether you should perform the deed or avoid it
1.	....	....	....	....
2.	....	....	....	....
3.	....	....	....	....
4.	....	....	....	....
5.	....	....	....	....
6.	....	....	....	....
7.	....	....	....	....
8.	....	....	....	....
9.	....	....	....	....
10.	....	....	....	....

Well, then, I'm sure you've taken a decisive step towards clearing confusion from your life by completing the chart above. However, your ultimate goal is to fully free yourself from confusion, and to achieve this, you must understand the design of Nature in its entirety. Let me reiterate that no matter what the action is or who performs it, it will always contain some flaw. Some 'wrong' will invariably result from every deed that is performed. In fact, I challenge those who constantly proclaim that one must 'do only good' to point out one such act that is completely devoid of negative consequence. I assure you, their lips will be sealed! So, disregard their claims. As for yourself, focus on keeping your intent pure at all times and choose the 'best possible deed' from the available options. Keep in mind that when you set out to do something good, some negativity will inevitably occur. Let it happen! You have no control over it, for this is the immutable design of Nature. Society and scriptures may shout their dictates and cry themselves hoarse, but they cannot alter this truth. So, do not waste your energy in such futile efforts. And neither must you burden yourself with the 'guilt' of committing a wrong, for you have not done any wrong intentionally. If you nurse such a guilt, it will only grow, taking on a far more dangerous form. Why don't you understand that psychology follows a sequence of events wherein an issue does not end with committing just one 'mistake'! In fact, it triggers many more automatically. First, you become confused due to the fear of doing something wrong and find yourself stuck in indecision, unsure whether to act. Then, in this state of confusion, you avoid the deeds that ought to be performed. And even if you do muster the courage to act or do so out of helplessness, you then carry the burden of guilt for your perceived wrong. But the problem doesn't end with guilt. You are well aware that this guilt haunts you for years, leading to even more mistakes. In short, this small piece of 'unnatural knowledge' of 'doing only good' has compelled the human being to commit countless mistakes. Honestly, all teachings that state, 'one must not engage in bad deeds' have only perplexed everyone endlessly. There is only one tenet of knowledge worth following: you must never intentionally commit any wrong, and this simple tenet encompasses everything.

Fortunately, you have now grasped the ultimate secret of Nature regarding *karma.* Therefore, release yourself from any confusion about good and bad *karma* once and for all. Continue engaging in good actions, whenever possible, without worrying about the bad that may result from them. Do not dwell on the negative or carry any guilt regarding it. Focus solely on 'the good you have done', because the fact remains that you have performed a good deed. Any bad that may have arisen is simply part of the process of doing the good deed.

Let me illustrate this with an example from the life of the multi-faceted personality, Krishna. After enunciating the profound Bhagavad Gita, what did Krishna do next? He fought in the brutal Mahabharata war. And what happened in that war? Unspeakable violence. What role did Krishna play in that violence? He spoke lies, broke vows and deceived many. Just think, after enunciating such a remarkable scripture, Krishna still engaged in such acts! However, this is an erroneous perception. To truly understand Krishna's actions, you must view them from his perspective. In the context of the Mahabharata war, Krishna's focus was entirely on one goal: reining in the sins perpetrated by the Kauravas. His aim was to ensure the Kauravas' defeat in the war. But why? To prevent the greater violence that would have resulted if the Kauravas had won the war. Krishna's focus was on the 'greater good',

'What will others say?' has become so problematic, it could easily be considered one of humanity's greatest burdens

ensuring that a far graver violence was averted in the future. This being the case, if you were to ask Krishna, "O supreme being, why did you lie, cheat and break vows?" his answer would be, "I have neither lied nor broken a vow. I simply did whatever was necessary to put an end to the depravity and sins of the Kauravas." But who would comprehend this? Misinterpreting his actions, people say, "Krishna broke his vow" or "Krishna made Yudhishthira lie." And such a misunderstanding is unfortunate indeed! These remarks are an insult to a great figure like Krishna. Ironically, it is often those who claim to love and revere him the most who make such remarks. This is why I state, this is the height of psychological ignorance. We live in an advanced, scientific era where we've made extraordinary discoveries about the human body, such as DNA and genes, and have even reached the Moon and the Mars. So, why can't we use psycho-spiritual knowledge to uncover the truths about human life and Nature? Why can't we comprehend the psychology of great personalities like Krishna? I am dedicated to this pursuit, and all I ask for is your support in this endeavour. Together, we can surely find solutions to the challenges facing humanity.

Indeed, if you can truly grasp the essence of what I've explained with the help of Krishna's example, you will fathom the entire game of Nature as well. Then, you will no longer be consumed by worry or burdened with guilt for having committed a wrong. You will begin performing all your *karmas* fearlessly, just as Krishna did, free from confusion. And that is exactly what you must do. Etch it in your mind that you have actually done good deeds; whatever bad has ensued is simply the result of the natural laws of *karma.* So, why

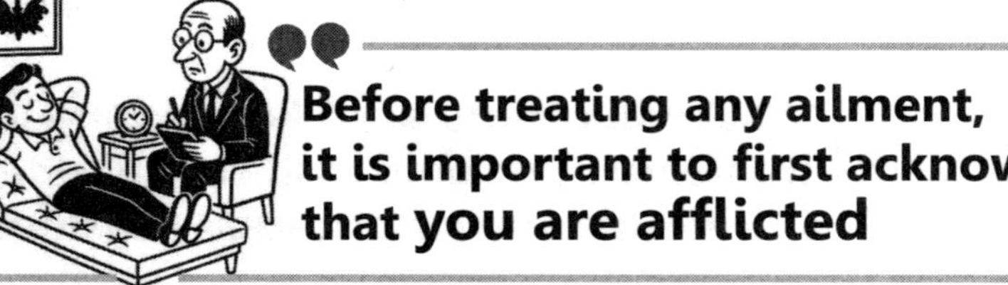

should we hold ourselves responsible for Nature's way of functioning? You can only be held accountable if your actions result in more harm than good. In fact, in such cases, you don't deserve to be forgiven at all. However, when the good of your actions outweighs the bad, there is no reason to worry about the negative outcome, because you did not intentionally cause the bad—it simply unfolded on its own.

Well, now that we have conversed at such length, let me draw your attention to an important aspect. Krishna remained joyful all his life, never carrying guilt or regret for anything he did. Why? Because he was answerable only to his soul. He never concerned himself with the opinions of society, religion or the world. The world could label him a liar or cheat, but Krishna was clear about his actions and the reasons behind them. And this is the mindset you must adopt as well! I have already shared with you the ultimate secret of Nature to help you become like Krishna. So, from today onwards, you must perform good deeds and live peacefully too. And if you truly wish to do both, then focus only on your soul and not on the world around you. Otherwise, you will always remain trapped in confusion, unable to perform good actions and burdened by unnecessary guilt. I have made every effort to help you eliminate the confusion surrounding 'good' and 'bad'; the onus is now on you to make a determined effort. Trust me, with this approach, you will surely find relief from this unnatural and harmful affliction called confusion!

Given the seriousness of this matter, allow me to make yet another attempt to free you from your confusion. I'm sure you are familiar with Buddha and Christ, but I would like to highlight their actions, as you may not have fully appreciated the significance of the great deeds they performed. Gautam Buddha was born into a Hindu family and grew up surrounded by the traditions and culture of Hinduism. However, when he gained enlightenment, he saw through the hypocrisies within Hinduism. And that was a turning point for him. He began speaking out vehemently against the fallacies in Hindu scriptures and practices. Undoubtedly, Buddha worked for the greater good by challenging these hypocrisies. But consider this: in that era, Hinduism was the only religion that existed in India, in which case, wouldn't those who were deeply devoted to their faith have suffered as a result of Buddha's outspoken criticism of their scriptures and traditions? Surely, their hearts must have ached! So, did Buddha commit a wrong by causing them to suffer this way? No, he did not! He only performed the good deed of eliminating hypocrisy—people were hurt as part of the process. Similarly, Jesus Christ was born into a Jewish family. When he attained knowledge, he too vigorously opposed the hypocrisies within Judaism. Upon deeper reflection, you'll see that even Christ's great work was the same as Buddha's: eliminating hypocrisy—the Jews were hurt only in the process of carrying out this 'great deed'. The point is, even in the greatest of actions, some negative outcomes are inevitable. However, you must understand this simple truth: 'fearing the bad', one cannot avoid performing good *karmas.* Once you truly grasp this, all your confusion will be dispelled. And with confusion gone, you will find yourself able to perform more and more deeds. The more deeds you perform, the more magnificent your life will become. At this point, I don't think there is any need to elaborate further on this simple math.

Although, in this context, it is essential to grasp a few more points, the most crucial being: in life, you cannot 'determine' the actions you will or won't perform. It is always 'life' that determines this. Life creates such diverse circumstances that you are compelled to fall in line with its dictates. What I mean is, those who try to impose their wishes on life will always end up straying from their path. So, kindly ensure you never engage in such futile efforts. Whatever life demands from you at any given moment, just act on it. Don't be stubborn like Arjuna, who, at the slightest pretext, would declare, 'I will not fight the war!' Understand that Krishna was there to guide Arjuna, which saved the latter, but it's up to you to protect yourself. Therefore, don't impose your own terms and conditions on life based on your 'misguided knowledge'. Know well that those who are ever ready to perform deeds as per the demands of life are the only ones who leave their mark on this world.

Let me expand on this further, as confusion is an age-old problem, and teachings about 'which actions to perform and which to avoid' have been around for centuries. Alright, tell me, what exactly are the teachings that advise one to 'do good' and 'avoid the bad' all about? Well, they are all about trying to choose your *'karma'* yourself. Please understand that neither of the above-mentioned teachings—'do good' and 'avoid the bad'—guide you to perform your *'karma'* as per the demands of life. They don't teach you to act as per 'time, opportunity and circumstances', whereas the truth is, only 'life' can determine which actions you must take and which ones you should avoid. After all, who can predict where life will steer you at any given moment! The simple, straightforward wisdom is that you must choose the 'best possible deed' keeping time, opportunity and circumstances in mind. And to make this choice, Nature has equipped every person with 'intelligence'. And really, what could be greater than intelligence? So, awaken your intelligence and pay heed to it. Your intelligence doesn't need guidance on which actions to take or avoid. After all, why would anyone need to teach their intelligence what is good or bad? To state this bluntly, those who impart flawed teachings are doubting your intelligence. And ironically, when you accept such ideas, your actions reflect your foolishness. Whereas, all you need to do is resolve never to intentionally commit a wrong. Once you have made this resolve, leave the rest to your intelligence. I fail to see

Clinging to thoughts that one realises are wrong is nothing but 'stubbornness'

how not using the incredible intelligence given to us by Nature could be considered religiousness or socially correct behaviour. Starting today, observe for yourself: those who refrain from using their intelligence are the very people who become religious or socially acceptable. This is a major hint I have provided, so grasp it well and become 'human' in the truest sense of the word. Understand that only those who use their own intelligence can truly be called human beings. Those who live off borrowed intelligence are merely puppets in the circus of life.

Honestly, in this context, both Krishna's life and the import of the Bhagavad Gita become essential. So, let me ask you: can you compile a list of actions—what to do and what to avoid—based on Krishna's life? Can you draw a clear distinction between what is good and what is bad from his life or from the Gita? In the Gita, Krishna elucidates, 'I am lust...I am anger...I am the ego...and also the monstrous form of 'kaal' (time), which I have taken on to devour and destroy all.' This being the case, tell me, will you be able to prepare a list of good-bad deeds from Krishna's life or from the Gita? The answer is no, you cannot. This is because the sole teaching of both Krishna and the Bhagavad Gita guides you towards 'using your intelligence'. Although I shouldn't be saying this, I will still point out that the majority of people are only engaged in efforts to 'dim your intelligence'. However, this is deeply flawed and is exactly why my discussions invariably revolve around Krishna and the Gita, forming the premise for most of my books as well.

Now, understand this: you are a human being equipped with remarkable intelligence. And this intelligence will never guide you to lie, steal or deceive. However, this

Confusing behaviour is no less dangerous than confusion itself

intelligence also recognises the complexities of life and, therefore, it doesn't simply take an oath to "refrain from doing bad" without considering the circumstances. Look at Arjuna, for example—why was he confused on the battlefield? It was because he was gripped with the fear of committing a wrong. And what advice did Krishna give him? Krishna questioned his cowardice and told him to rise above it. Unfortunately, all the futile knowledge around us today feeds into this very cowardice, which is why it's crucial to break free from it. You too must become like the brave and valiant Krishna. If kidnappers were to abduct your child, wouldn't you thrash them to protect your child? In moments like these, you must not allow yourself to be paralysed by the fear of "doing wrong". Never think, "How can I thrash someone or how can I commit violence?"

To sum up, you have to build the capability and confidence in yourself that 'Yes, I can do anything!' Intentionally, you must never commit any wrong, and that is why you must not fear anything considering it to be wrong. Trust your intelligence and use it optimally. And whenever life offers you a choice, continue choosing the best possible option. It is pointless to concern yourself with what religion, society, family members or the so-called wise have to say. The truth is, no one can understand your life better than you do. Hence, it is only you who can truly determine which actions to take and why. And to help you decide this, Nature has equipped you with intelligence. Moreover, you are answerable to your inner self only. So, what's the need for elaborate lists of "dos and don'ts"? Simply reflect on Krishna's life, internalise the true import of the Gita, and watch how your cowardice vanishes in no time. Once your intelligence is fully awakened, confusion about your actions or your life will be gone for good. I hope that, having understood this, you will no longer be confused about the concepts of 'good' and 'bad'.

Freedom from Confusion Demands a Price!

We have fully grasped one of the prime reasons behind confusion and have also come to understand that *karma* is inherently 'flawed', meaning, it is impossible to perform an action that produces purely good outcomes. And since it's impossible to perform a deed that yields only good, there's no reason to fear the potential bad outcomes either. Of course, we must be cautious not to intentionally commit harm, but we should not let the fear of possible negative consequences prevent us from carrying out the actions we must. We shouldn't think, "If I do this, it will lead to that wrong." We need to understand that a 'significant amount of good' is also occurring as a result of the bad deed. Given that every action inevitably involves some degree of bad, we must move forward without confusion, choosing to perform the deeds wherein the good outweighs the bad. That's it! With this approach, you will forever be liberated from the 'confusion regarding good and bad'.

Now, let's explore the second major cause of confusion. But to do so, we must first understand the game of life. So, tell me, what is the game of life all about? Having lived for this long, you should already have some sense of the answer. But let me outline it for you. The game of life is simple: in this world, nothing comes for free. To gain anything in this world, you must pay a price for it. Unfortunately, most people fail to recognise this basic truth, and this lack of understanding is the second leading cause of confusion.

Alright, let me ask you this: why do only a few individuals make significant progress in life while the vast majority grapples with failure? Surely, there must be a reason. After all, when we compare people physically, there's hardly any difference. Everyone makes efforts and no one lacks the desire. So, why are so many people's lives entangled in problems? Have you ever thought about this? If not, why haven't you? At the very least, you should have considered why only a handful of people seem to succeed in the game of life. It's fine if you haven't reflected on this before, but kindly do not resort to vague or unfounded explanations. I speak to you from a scientific and psychologically accurate perspective, grounded in spiritual principles... and anything outside that framework is not the truth anyway. So, I won't discuss anything else and I suggest that you too refrain from entertaining irrelevant discussions.

For now, let us return to the fundamental question: why is it that only a small number of people achieve remarkable feats in life while the majority continues to struggle despite making persistent efforts? It is only because the latter group is trapped in confusion. But what exactly is confusion? It is the mindset where people expect to gain everything for 'free'. They don't want to pay the price to acquire anything. Take a moment to reflect. You too may recognise within yourself the greed to acquire things without paying the price. And it is precisely this greed that leads people down the path of ruination. No one is willing to accept that this is simply not possible as per the law of Nature. As I've mentioned before, everything in Nature operates according to its own laws, and the laws of life are no exception. And the ultimate law of life states that nothing in this world can be acquired for free. There is no way around this law. However, the problem is that this law does not apply to 'desires'—it applies to 'results'. What this means is that while it's fine to wish for something without wanting to pay the price, the outcome of that desire is governed by Nature's laws.

The reality is that everyone wants to accomplish great things, but out of the fear of paying the price, they are unable to perform the 'deeds' that will lead to the accomplishment of those desires. As soon as they are struck with the thought, "What price will I have to pay for this?" they become confused. The moment they think, "I will suffer a loss," they put the *karma* on 'hold' because no one wants to actually pay the price. This is something that happens with most people several times a day. I urge you too, to observe this in yourself from today onwards—how often do you put your deeds on hold due to the fear of paying the price? Bear in mind that I am discussing the ultimate secret of life, so read each and every word carefully. If you haven't fully grasped it, read it again. If you miss this opportunity, you will never be able to free yourself from confusion, for it is this very confusion that entangles your life in a multitude of problems. So, understand clearly that you cannot gain anything in life for 'free'. To achieve anything, you must be willing to pay the price, regardless of what you have set out to achieve. This is how the arrangement of 'gain and loss' works in life as determined by Nature, and we are all bound to live by this arrangement.

I understand that you may find this hard to believe at first, and it may take some time for you to fully grasp this concept—and that's perfectly fine. One should not rush when trying to comprehend something deeply, and it is important not to agree with anything until you have a clear and thorough understanding of it. However, let me point out that you are not entirely unaware of this 'law of life'. When you purchase something from a store, you don't hesitate to pay the price, because you know that every product in the market carries a price and you won't be able to acquire it without paying its price. You may try to bargain, but you never ask anyone to give you the product for 'free' because you're fully aware that in a marketplace, asking for a free product is considered as begging. In other words, you are absolutely clear that you will not receive anything for free in a 'market that sells goods'. You are not confused as far as the market of material objects is concerned. Hence, you unreservedly purchase products in exchange for a price, without getting confused at all, for you are completely clear that in today's era, you cannot even secure the blessings of God without paying money for it!

But what you may not realise is that life is not limited to just transactions i.e. paying a price and purchasing goods, for this exchange amounts to just five percent of your life. The real exchanges in life are far greater than this, and it is in these that you experience the most difficulties, for they do not entail a fixed price. In such exchanges, you do not have to pay 'monetarily', and barring money, you are totally clueless about the 'practical exchanges of life', because no one teaches you the psychology underlying them. As a result, you are unaware that every exchange in life carries a price, and that no exchange is possible without paying the price for it.

To sum it up, you are unaware of the reality of life that there is a certain 'price' for every kind of exchange, and more significantly, you do not even wish to pay the price in the other exchanges of life. Whereas it is the irrevocable law of life that in any kind of 'exchange', you cannot acquire anything without paying its price. Unfortunately, the vast majority is clueless about this.

Well, now that you have understood this fundamental concept, let me ask you: what is life? Life, in its essence, is a series of exchanges where every gain portends

Every person inherently has three core desires which are his 'lifeline'

a loss, and every loss makes room for gain. In simpler terms, it is impossible to 'gain' anything without 'losing' something. And for life to function harmoniously or even to create a splendid life, everyone has to constantly engage in these exchanges. Consider something as basic as breathing. In exchange for the oxygen we inhale, we must "pay the price" by exhaling carbon dioxide. So, just think, if even something as basic as breathing is an exchange, then it is clear that no other exchanges in life can be one-sided.

In short, every exchange in life is a process of 'give-and-take'. So, what does that make life? A 'business'. And in business, who succeeds and thrives? It's the person who pays a lesser price in exchange for items of greater value. Now, if someone refuses to participate in exchanges out of the fear that they will have to pay a price for it, what will happen to their business? It will stagnate. And this is the key to understanding why many people fail in life—the fear of paying the price for what they want leads them to shut down their 'shop of exchanges'. If you're struggling to carve a splendid life, it's because the very thought of paying the price overwhelms you with confusion. Greed, or the fear of losing something, often paralyses people into inaction. Think about it: if someone wants to breathe but refuses to exhale carbon dioxide, what would happen? They wouldn't even be able to continue reading this book! Thus, you must accept that acquiring anything without paying its price is simply not possible as per the law of Nature. If you fail to understand this, then you're bound to ruin your "life-business". Honestly, the fear of paying the price is what holds most people back from thriving; otherwise building a great life does not require extraordinary effort.

The death of one's personality is no different from one's actual death

Well, you are intelligent and I've already given you a clue. I hope that from this moment onwards, you will steer clear of the confusion resulting from the misconception that you can acquire something without paying its price. You'll realise that 'give-and-take' is the essence of all transactions, whether in a retail store or in the practical world of exchanges. To purchase goods from a store, you will have to pay money, and in 'the practical world of exchanges', you will have to pay a price either in 'mental or physical' terms. In short, you will never attain anything for free anywhere—this is the unchangeable law of life. So, from now on, don't hesitate to pay the price. Your only resolve should be to garner as many items as you can from the bazaar of life. Since you have been granted the gift of human life, make a resolve that you will acquire the finest things and experiences this world has to offer; fearing the price, you will not live a dull and boring life.

In short, you must live your life in a spectacular manner just like Krishna. Despite being born in a dungeon, Krishna enjoyed life in all its myriad hues. He relished a simple meal with just butter in it as much as he savoured the lavish *Chhappan Bhog* (a meal comprising 56 food items). He showered his love on Radha and celebrated the *raas* with the gopis. He adorned himself in the finest attire and jewellery and even went on to establish the magnificent city of Dwarka. Is there any pleasure in life—be it dancing or playing the flute—that Krishna did not savour? Though a humble cowherd, he married eight times, and the majority of his wives were princesses. He made the mightiest kings and kingdoms dance to his tune. And above all, he gave humanity the Bhagavad Gita—the most profound wisdom in the history of mankind. This begs the question: did Krishna receive all these incredible experiences from the bazaar of life for free? No, he paid the price for everything. And he did so without hesitation or confusion, because he fully understood the law of life that nothing can be gained without paying a price for it. This is why Krishna was able to 'garner' so much from life and revel in its many splendid hues. Actually, whether it is the Gita or Krishna's life, nothing in this world is more significant than these two.

Now, let us return to the central point of our discussion: those who fear paying the price or try to gain something without paying the price are forever confused. And this confusion prevents them from performing the deeds that are necessary to acquire what they want from the bazaar of life. This means, due to this tiny bit of confusion, they are stuck living a dull and boring life. Simply put, nothing in this world comes for free, so you must never shy away from paying the price. Life is a business, so you must treat it as one. And in any business, the goal is to grow and expand. A business thrives and expands only when you pay a lesser price for goods of greater value. In life too, you must try to become a successful businessman by seeking to acquire the best that it has to offer in exchange for a smaller price. Just keep engaging in this process and over time, your life will automatically brim over with rich and vibrant experiences. But yes, you must never acquire anything that costs more than its worth. Always be cautious just as you would when making a business deal, and you will see the "balance sheet" of your life start to reflect profit.

I suspect that many of you may not have fully understood what 'paying the price' truly means. So, let's break it down for clarity. We all know that to live a good life, money is necessary. At the same time, everyone knows that money does not grow on trees. In other words, money will not come to you without paying a price. So, what's the price? It's a combination of 'hard work' and 'acumen'. But if someone believes they can earn money without putting in the effort or using their acumen, will they succeed? Clearly, no. The same principle applies to every aspect of life. Consider marriage, for example. Everyone desires a life partner, and many eagerly marry. However, most people mistakenly assume that they will receive a life partner "for free". But that's not the reality. A life partner comes at the cost of sacrifices, particularly those concerning your personal freedom. The frequent squabbles that arise...that's also a kind of price one pays. And sometimes, you have to take on additional responsibilities too. All of this amounts to the 'price' you have to pay to get a life partner.

In short, one does not get even a life partner without paying a price for it. So, if you enter marriage thinking you're getting a partner for free, you'll surely regret it later. For, when it's time to pay the price, you may wonder, "Why did I get married?" But that regret is also nothing but the fear of paying the price. In fact, it only proves that you were unaware of what marriage would cost. And truly, to enter a deal without knowing its 'price' is sheer foolishness, and it is only such fools who end up cribbing and lamenting their decisions. However, the wise do not engage in such idiocies. They are well aware that in order to acquire anything, they will have to pay a price. So, before they strike a deal, they first weigh all the pros and cons and assess what they want to attain and the price they will have to pay for it. If what they are getting seems more valuable than its price, they proceed. You too must develop this wisdom and accept the reality that nothing in this world is available for free. And since you are not receiving anything for free, to refrain from purchasing items of value out of the fear of paying their price is also sheer foolishness. Similarly, purchasing a product without being aware of its price and bringing it home also amounts to foolishness. Sadly, many people make these two mistakes day in and day out. The first mistake will deprive you of valuable goods, while the second mistake will make you regret your decision of acquiring the goods. This is the very reason why such people

Because most people have lost touch with their desires, the world feels full of 'living corpses'

become 'bankrupt' in the business of life. So, to save yourself from this fate, firstly, you must not be afraid to pay the price. Secondly, you must not harbour the misconception that you will get anything for free. Most importantly, never purchase anything without knowing its true price. If even something as essential as oxygen demands something in exchange, nothing else in life will come for free either.

If I were to share a secret, it is that confusion in human beings does not arise because they are ignorant about the law that nothing can be procured for free. Truth be told, a human being, by nature, is extremely 'greedy'. He desires everything this world has to offer, but he wants it without giving anything in return. In fact, it is this very 'tendency of greed' in a human being that has dimmed his intelligence, leading him to misunderstand the game of life. As a result, most people are afraid to pay the price, even though the undeniable truth remains: nothing in this world comes for free. And this is why entire lives are spent in confusion. People want everything, but they do not want to pay its price. So, instead of acting on it, they sit back, overthink and worry, caught up in endless talk but no action. This has become the default state for many, leading them to live a dull and drab life without any achievements to their name.

However, you must comprehend that life is about living wholeheartedly and garnering everything to your heart's desire. And if you want to live such a life, you must be ready to pay the price. You are equipped with everything, from physical strength to a mind and intellect, to work hard and pay the price. So, use your body where physical effort is needed, apply your brain for strategic thinking, and exercise prudence where required. If you can achieve something through patience and peace, then maintain those qualities...especially when dealing with your spouse, as they are key to success in such relationships. Above all, be willing to pay the price with a smile on your face and even sacrifice your freedom occasionally, if needed. Comprehend clearly that to achieve something extraordinary, sometimes, you have to take a risk or even endure mental stress. But no matter what, remember that nothing in this world comes for free. Nature has given you an able body, sharp mind and keen senses, all of which enable you to pay the price for what you want. So, why should you be afraid to pay the price when you're fully equipped to do so? Holding onto the greed of wanting everything without paying its price is frankly disgraceful. So, let go of such foolish notions. Understand that in exchange for the price you pay, you are receiving far more in return. So, whether it's enduring your spouse's taunts or sulks, bear them with a smile. After all, in exchange for this small cost, you are gaining an invaluable life partner.

So, you must never crib or cry or allow frustration or sadness to take root in your life. Understand clearly that to even enjoy your favourite meal, you have to pay a price. That price could come in the form of a stomach ache or weight gain. In other words, everything you wish to attain, no matter how simple or ordinary, entails some or other cost. This being the case, you can't spend your entire life trying to evade the price that you have to pay. Fearing the price that life demands, you surely cannot renounce the world and live a solitary life in the Himalayas. Once you fully understand this, you will unlock the ability to achieve many things in life, and that too happily, sporting a broad smile on your face.

In essence, since life is a business, we must treat it as one. Never let an opportunity to pay a lesser price for something greater in value slip by. When you come across such an opportunity, don't hesitate at all. Seize it quickly and reap the rewards. The math is simple: if you can acquire something worth Rs 80 for the price of Rs 20, you're making a profit of Rs 60. If someone then complains about losing the Rs 20 they spent to gain it, they've surely lost their mind! And anyone who rejects Rs 80 worth of value out of fear of losing Rs 20 is truly misguided. However, you must never behave in such a way. From this moment on, eliminate all confusion and actively pursue everything you can by paying a lesser price. Then, just watch how your life's balance sheet becomes more and more profitable, and how the world marvels at your achievements. However, there is one more caution you need to consider. Since nothing in life comes for free, never try to gain anything without first assessing its price. Don't ever assume you will get something for nothing. Before you set out to acquire anything, ensure you're fully aware of the price you'll need to pay. Only if the price seems reasonable should you move forward. It should never be the case that you acquire something first and realise its price only later—that will only lead to regret. Indeed, if you discover later that the price is steep, you'll end up with a loss in the balance sheet of your life. What's worse, because you didn't understand the cost upfront, you'll face the added burden of "suddenly" having to pay the price. To put it simply, just because you picked something up assuming it was free, doesn't mean you'll get away without paying for it. If you make such an assumption, you'll find yourself regretting your actions when the time comes to pay the price. And we definitely don't want to engage in such foolishness.

Practical Application

Alright! Let me provide you with an exercise to help you eliminate all confusion regarding this. In the chart below, assess and fill in the 'price' and 'value' of the ten most important things you are currently pursuing. Then, looking at the 'price', evaluate whether each item is truly worth pursuing based on the value you've assigned to it. In fact, I recommend keeping multiple copies of this chart as well as all other practical applications given in this book handy. Once you've filled out one chart, continue the process in a fresh copy. For every new exchange you encounter, fill in the chart and assess whether it is something worth pursuing. This exercise will at least help you start procuring things based on a clear understanding of the price you're paying. Moreover, it will instantly eliminate confusion about whether to pursue something or not. With time, this process will not only clear up confusion, but also ensure there won't be a pause in your *karmas.* So, take full advantage of the practical applications shared in this book and use them to live a confusion-free life, elevating it to new heights.

No.	Describe what you want to attain	Its value according to you	The price you have to pay to attain it	Decide whether you want to attain it or not
1.	....	....	....	....
2.	....	....	....	....
3.	....	....	....	....
4.	....	....	....	....
5.	....	....	....	....
6.	....	....	....	....
7.	....	....	....	....
8.	....	....	....	....
9.	....	....	....	....
10.	....	....	....	....

So far, we have established that achieving anything in this world requires paying a price. To delve deeper into this point, let's take an example from the Bhagavad Gita. You might wonder why I refer to the Gita so often; well, the reason is simple: both the consciousness of Krishna and the profundity of the Bhagavad Gita are truly remarkable. Gita is not just a scripture but an immensely profound psychology as well. It baffles me that most people have never explored its psychological dimensions! Although many are familiar with its spiritual teachings, the psychological depth of the Gita remains largely unexplored, but truth be told, its psychological aspects are just as significant as its spiritual depth. That is why I have written two books on the Bhagavad Gita—one titled 'I am Gita' which captures the essence of all 18 chapters, and the other which offers a detailed, sequential explanation of all 700 shlokas. And in both books, I have explained the spiritual and psychological aspects of the Gita in detail.

Now, returning to our main point, I'm sure you are familiar that the Gita commences with Arjuna being in a state of confusion, unsure whether to fight the war or not. He says to Krishna, "I am completely perplexed. I cannot determine which option is better—fighting the war or not. I don't know which of the two is more beneficial for me." This means Arjuna is totally confused, and one of the reasons for his predicament is that he is unable to decide which of the two options is more beneficial for him. Krishna then explains to him that neither option will bring him complete benefit. After all, war, by nature, leads to destruction. Thus, seeking a benefit from war is a folly in itself. Krishna tells Arjuna, "You must realise that if the situation has escalated to this point and

To live free of confusion is the very purpose of life, for only then can a human being reach his destination

culminated in a war, you have played a major role in it. You could have avoided this conflict earlier, but now, with the situation out of control, you can no longer choose between benefit and harm. The real choice is between lesser harm and greater harm." This is a key lesson for all of us too: in life, you won't always come across situations where you have a clear choice between benefit and harm. Often, you will have to choose between lesser harm and greater harm. And it is at this point that a person slips deeper into confusion, resulting in even more disastrous outcomes. Well, I'm sure you can now see that the Gita is uniquely equipped to explain such complex subjects, which is why I refer to it so often. Besides, the theme of this book is confusion, and the Gita begins with Arjuna caught in the throes of confusion.

Well, let us now dive deeper into Krishna's advice to Arjuna, who found himself torn between two choices, standing in the midst of the battlefield. Krishna made it clear that since the matter pertains to war, and that too, a war of such magnitude, one does not have the liberty to choose between benefit and harm. The only real choice is between 'lesser harm' and 'greater harm'. For Arjuna, the lesser harm is in fighting the war. Of course, by choosing to fight, he faces the inevitable risk of death, which is a likely outcome in any war. In fact, anyone who seeks to avoid that risk should never engage in a battle in the first place. However, since Arjuna is already in that situation, he must accept the possibility of death and move forward. Well, just as Krishna's advice to Arjuna holds significance, this lesson is crucial for you as well. If you are afraid to fight, don't let any situation spiral and escalate to a fight. But if you are already in the thick of it and have no choice but to face it, don't only focus on the potential benefit. In any conflict, the only real choice is between 'lesser harm' and 'greater harm'. In such crucial moments, don't act like Arjuna. Arjuna had Krishna to guide him, but you only have your own intelligence to rely on. Unfortunately, many people fail to use their intelligence effectively, perhaps preferring to keep it unused just as they found it.

The important point is that, unlike Arjuna, you don't have Krishna by your side. So, the only way you can safeguard yourself from confusion is by using your intelligence. Besides, you have no option but to do so, for confusion indicates a state of indecisiveness, which means putting the *karma* on hold; and one cannot afford to be in an 'indecisive state' in the midst of a war. Now, consider this: your actions are on hold because you are confused, but that does not stop the other person...because he is not confused about the action he should take. Just think, has Nature stopped functioning just because you are confused? Arjuna may be unable to decide whether to fight the war or not, but Duryodhana is not confused at all. Had Arjuna continued to remain confused, Duryodhana would have killed him at the very outset of the war. In other words, a confused Arjuna would have met an untimely end. However, since Krishna was standing by Arjuna's side, he was saved. But you must become your own protector and save yourself from ruin. And to do that, you must get rid of confusion at any cost, otherwise you will meet an 'untimely death' repeatedly. Also, this lesson isn't limited to just war. Whether you're facing a battle fought with weapons or any other challenge, confusion is perilous. For, confusion leads to inaction, and a life without action is a life that cannot progress. Therefore, never treat confusion lightly. Remember, even a minor confusion is capable of pushing you into the bottomless pit of ruin.

Now, let's return to Krishna's response to Arjuna. When a confused Arjuna bombarded Krishna with questions, Krishna said, "If you fight, there is a chance you might die...but there is also a chance you might win. If you win, you will gain a kingdom. However, this gain is not without its own cost—many will perish, including your own kinsmen. So, while you may gain something, the war will also bring great harm. Yet, this is the one and only alternative you have. On the other hand, if you flee the battlefield, the harm will be even greater. First, you will be seen as a coward and your honour will be tarnished. For a warrior of your stature, such shame and dishonour will be intolerable. Second, if you flee, your army will lose the war and your brothers and sons may die in the process, leaving you to grieve their deaths forever. Moreover, imagine how severely Draupadi will rebuke you! In short, you need to realise that if you fight the war, you might die once, but if you flee the battlefield, you will die a thousand deaths every day. Therefore, Arjuna, the best course of action is to fight because that would bring the least amount of harm for you, and also some possibility of 'gain'. In fact, let me acquaint you with one more reality. If you remain in this state of confusion and the war commences, you will die without even fighting, and your death will be in vain." Well, just like Arjuna, you too must remember that if you remain confused in a conflict and choose not to act, you will meet your end for no reason. That is why I state that the confusion that grips you in the midst of a fight brings the most disastrous results, and this is why Krishna repeatedly advises Arjuna in the Gita, "O Arjuna, rid yourself of confusion and stand up and fight the war. The war brings the possibility of death, but it also offers the chance to win. However, if you remain caught in confusion, you will die without even the possibility of a positive outcome." This illustrates just how dangerous confusion can be in the midst of a battle! It also highlights how the teachings of the Gita make it easier to grasp deep and complex truths.

Now, let's approach this entire matter from a fresh perspective, because risking your whole life due to confusion is not prudent at all. It is amply clear that the entire cosmos functions in accordance with laws. Every 'visible' and 'invisible' entity in this world, including human life, is governed by its own set of laws. So, let

Only someone who discovers the purpose of his life i.e. his 'personal goal' can triumph over confusion

me ask you this: how can anyone succeed in the game of life without understanding its laws? It is simply impossible.

So, the first question to consider is: what exactly is the game of life? Because to win any game, you need to know the game and its rules. In simple terms, the game of life revolves around gain and loss. A human being starts playing this game from the moment he is born till he breathes his last. This is basically what life is all about. With that in mind, if someone expects only gain without any loss, that's simply not possible. In short, life is a 'give-and-take', essentially a business, and a business only thrives when you give less and receive more in exchange. If you pay a higher price and gain less in return, you'll undoubtedly face losses and fall behind in the business of life. And if you're afraid to pay the price for something, you will not be able to make progress at all.

So, to carve a grand life, you must wholeheartedly engage in this business till your last breath without being bogged down by confusion. Here, it is also important to understand that in the business of life, not every action is performed with the intent of making money. Life necessitates countless exchanges that are inevitable. Pursuing your hobbies, interests and passions is also one such exchange. Let's look at an example. Someone who consumes alcohol in moderation might derive more joy in exchange for a lesser price, but those who indulge excessively inevitably suffer in the long run. The takeaway is that your hobbies and interests are also a kind of exchange, so approach them as you would a business transaction. The same applies to striking up friendships, organising social gatherings, maintaining relationships or any other form of interaction. Every action carries a price. Your mind might crave spicy food, but in exchange,

As long as an ocean of options exists, confusion will exist too

your body may suffer from acidity. On the other hand, if you choose bland food, your body will stay healthy but your mind may feel unsatisfied. In other words, in life, you must always pay some price for everything you do, because to gain anything in life, you must engage in exchanges. And since you have to engage in give-and-take, remember that you must give less and receive more. Once you learn to do this consistently without any confusion, your life will be set in no time.

Now that we have explored this topic in depth, let's reflect on one more key point: life is a 'never-ending process' that begins at birth and ends with death. In the interim, life does not stop, even for a moment. Whether you are experiencing stress, illness or facing untold hardships, life continues without pause. And if life never halts, neither should you. Just as your 'business' of breathing—inhaling oxygen and exhaling carbon dioxide—remains uninterrupted until your last breath, the other 'businesses' of your life must also continue ceaselessly, free from confusion. The flow of your life, just like your breath, should never stop. And only when this happens can a grand life be carved. For, just as the thread of life snaps if the 'business of breathing' were to stop, the progress of life comes to a standstill when the thread of the other businesses of life breaks. If the world is rife with failures, it is only because the thread of everyone's life-business is getting stuck time and again. And why is it getting stuck? It is only because of confusion. Questions such as, "Should I do this?" or "What should I do?" create a paralysis that halts progress. And needless to say, as stagnant water breeds decay, a life that ceases to flow stagnates inevitably and loses its vitality.

Thus, the 'business of life' must continue unabated from the moment of birth to the moment of death. In fact, the reality of life is such that a human being has to engage in profitable interactions even on his deathbed—otherwise, he cannot even die a 'peaceful death'. For instance, it is perfectly fine to stop pursuing wealth once you've secured enough savings, for a lifetime can be lived on the strength of savings. But this is not the case in the other aspects of life, which have to be dealt with till your last breath. In such cases, it becomes imperative for all such exchanges to continue ceaselessly, without confusion. And this is possible only when you continue to garner more benefits in exchange for a lesser price, without harbouring any confusion.

But sadly, this is rarely the case! For one reason or the other, the exchanges of life invariably come to a halt. Truth be told, I have observed the majority of people living in a perpetual state of confusion only due to the fear of paying the price. This breeds confusion which ultimately robs them of some of the most valuable things they could have attained. Therefore, I urge you to become a 'daring businessperson' in the marketplace called life and pay every price happily, with a smile on your face. Consider this: if your partner tends to your needs, loves you, prepares meals and looks after the household, but occasionally becomes upset or throws a tantrum, is it a sin on their part? Of course not! So, instead of resenting it, approach it with a smile, understanding fully well that nothing in life is truly free. And since you are not getting anything for free, why should you be afraid of paying the price? Once you grasp this simple principle, you'll no longer be bogged down by confusion, nor will there be a break or pause on your exchanges. And this is essential to live a magnificent life. You must comprehend that the things that can be bought with money and the ones you get in exchange for your conduct are completely different. And both are essential to live a complete life.

Thus, I hope, from this day onwards, you will engage in both material and non-material exchanges with clarity and without hesitation. Seize every opportunity to pay a lesser price and gain something of greater value, and do so cheerfully. Never fear paying the price and do not complain or regret it either. Above all, rid yourself of the misconception that you can get anything in life for free. Once you understand this, you'll be freed from the second biggest cause of confusion. Then, just watch how your life comes alive with action—and action implies growth and progress. I am confident that hereon, your life will take a remarkable turn and the world will be amazed by your achievements. Indeed, a confusion-free life attains such phenomenal feats that one day, the entire world salutes it.

Last but not the least, let me emphasise that to build a spectacular life, you must perform *karma*, but it is impossible to do so in a confused state of mind. Every bit of knowledge pertaining to 'you must perform one action and avoid another' turns out to be ludicrous because it forces a human being to decide which actions he should perform and which he must refrain from. When, in fact, it is 'life' that determines when a person should engage in a certain action and when he should refrain from it. So, let life determine the actions you must undertake and the ones you must avoid. In the flow of life, whenever you have the opportunity, choose the 'best possible deed'—and 'best possible' implies a deed with a greater amount of good and less amount of bad. It signifies a *karma* wherein the gain outweighs the loss. So, persist in this endeavour until your last breath. Don't waste time looking back or checking the lists of good and bad—simply flow with life, free from confusion. Doing this, you will achieve greatness and your name will be etched in the annals of history. I've shared with you the most profound 'psychological science' of life, and believe me, Nature has given us this life only so that we can live it spectacularly. This is an incredible science, which once fathomed, makes all other knowledge unnecessary. I am confident that you will make the most of this simple solution I have shared and use it to your fullest advantage.

Mind–Brain Conflict

Biggest Cause of Confusion

So far, we have identified two primary causes of confusion and we shall now proceed to the third—the conflict between the mind and brain, which is yet another significant reason behind confusion. Now, both the mind and brain are present within us, yet most people are ignorant of the fundamental difference between the two. This is precisely why I repeatedly state that it is the ignorance about psychology that is hindering man's growth and progress. Despite acquiring vast amounts of knowledge and making all possible efforts, what do we see happening? Nothing significant! This is because without a deep understanding of psychology, it is impossible to achieve all-round success in all spheres of life. And without the knowledge of psycho-spirituality, one's challenges will only multiply. Please note that I'm not downplaying the importance of other subjects, but all that knowledge will prove useful only when you have a solid grasp of psychology and spirituality. Countless talented people fail to make significant strides in life, not because they lack ability, but because they lack the understanding of these two subjects. And I don't want you to belong to that ilk. Despite having potential, I don't want you to continue to suffer the hard knocks of life. So, comprehend clearly that to carve a spectacular life, understanding psychology and spirituality is just as important as talent and hard work.

Now, let's return to the matter at hand—confusion. As I've already pointed out, one of the primary reasons for confusion lies in the 'conflict' between the 'mind and brain'. But before we comprehend the basic difference between the two, it is important to first understand the 'science of *karma*'. Since you engage in countless *karmas* every day, you likely have some familiarity with the concept. So, tell me—who is performing all the *karmas* you engage in? I'm sure you would say, "the body". But the body doesn't really have the authority or power to perform significant deeds. I find it astounding that even after all these years, many have failed to recognise this simple truth. Just think: how will you steer your life in the right direction if you fail to recognise even your own system?

Comprehend clearly that the body doesn't have the power to perform even one great deed on its own. It is only free to perform basic functions like breathing and digesting food. Beyond that, the body is driven entirely by the desires of four forces: mind, brain, senses and ego. Think of these four as the masters of your body, much like multiple owners of a single shop. Now, it wouldn't matter whether there are four owners or forty as long as their desires are aligned—but the problem is, the desires of these four forces often clash. The senses yearn for sensory pleasures like tasty food and pleasant scents. The ego wants to appear "good" in the eyes of others and make a favourable impression on them, while the brain makes efforts to fulfil the desires stemming from the ego. And as far as the 'mind' is concerned, it is only interested in living blissfully and seeking the little joys of life. Most importantly, it values 'joy and concentration' above everything else. What I've just shared with you is the complete science of your inner system, which is indeed a rare opportunity to fathom profound wisdom. So, from today onwards, I encourage you to recognise the four masters of your system and understand that their desires are distinct from each other. This awareness will go a long way in making the journey of your life smooth and seamless.

Well, by now, you must have realised that the urge to perform a deed originates from within, and the body simply carries out the commands it receives. If you want to further comprehend the complete science of your inner system, read my book 'The Black Book of Soul'. At present though, comprehend well that there are four forces existent within you that compel you to perform actions. And since all four have varied desires, the orders given by each one of them to the body also vary. Having grasped this, you must have realised that this is where the matter becomes complicated i.e. when all four forces start issuing commands at the same time. And when this happens, you become confused about whom you should listen to. Picture this: what would happen if four people tried to ride a single horse and each steered it in a different direction? The horse will be totally confused about which direction to take and which master to obey. Your body also faces the same dilemma when all its four masters issue commands at the same time. Pay close attention to this dynamic from now on, and you'll realise that you experience this confusion multiple times throughout the day. In fact, since the subject is both significant and profound, I suggest you spend an entire day in solitude to clearly identify the four masters of your body. Trust me, once you engage in such deep introspections, your life will be transformed in no time. Opportunities for such deep reflection don't come easily, so seize them when you can.

Coming back to the key point, this is your inner system as 'determined by Nature', and as you know, no one has the authority to interfere with the workings of Nature. This means, you cannot remove the mind, brain, ego or senses from your inner framework, nor can you make these four masters issue only one command at a time. Your body will continue to receive commands from these four forces, each with their own agenda. At this point, you might think, "No wonder we're always confused!" But the truth is, you don't have to be. It is complex, yes, but by increasing your psychological awareness, you can overcome it. And it is important to free your mind from confusion, as you cannot allow it to disrupt the smooth flow of life. So, we will address this complicated cause of confusion too, but to do so, you need to sharpen your psychological insight and comprehend matters with the same depth and clarity with which I'm explaining them to you. And indeed, for a person with an evolved consciousness in today's scientific age, this is entirely possible.

For now, let us understand the confusion caused by the commands of the four masters. The desires of your senses are trivial and relatively insignificant. They don't create serious confusion, so you need not spend time and energy suppressing them. Really, what's the harm if your senses insist on you savouring certain foods or drinks or indulging in a little fun and frolic? Teachings that promote suppressing the senses might be considered pious, but you must seek solutions only in profound, psycho-spiritual principles. Allow your senses to indulge in their innocent desires without interference; otherwise, you'll only stir confusion and be deprived of the joys of life, all the while trying to be pious. So, do not commit this mistake. This is a compelling hint I have given you, and it is only for your betterment that I am doing this.

Now, let us focus on the brain and ego, which must be addressed together. Though they are separate forces, they often become a single force, each fuelling the other's desires. In many people, the brain and ego merge to such an extent that it becomes difficult to differentiate between them. Thus, to comprehend the matter at present, consider them as one cohesive unit, which leaves the final entity—your mind. To understand better the difference between the mind and brain-ego and experience the individual existence of both, I suggest reading my book 'I am The Mind'. For now, know

Most people are not even aware that decisions can be made without deliberation

that the mind and the combined unit of the brain and ego are the two main forces which 'command your actions'. This implies that all important commands regarding 'which actions you must perform or avoid' are either given by your 'mind' or the combined unit of your 'brain and ego'. And the most dangerous aspect is that most of the time, their commands contradict each other. This internal conflict is precisely why you become perplexed in almost every situation. Most importantly, both entities are extremely powerful and obstinate, making it difficult for you to ignore or suppress them. Truth be told, the 'conflicts' between the mind and brain-ego are so dangerous that they are solely responsible for ruining countless lives. However, you must prevail over this internal struggle because the confusion that arises as a consequence of this struggle is highly detrimental. This is why the great Indian poet, Kabir once said, "None remains unscathed when caught between two millstones," which is an apt metaphor for the destructive nature of the struggle between the mind and the brain-ego.

Well, no matter how powerful or dangerous these two millstones i.e. opposing forces may be, we must not ruin our lives by getting crushed between them. To triumph over this internal conflict, it is crucial to understand the desires emanating from both the mind and the brain-ego in detail. The good news is that, despite their conflicts, both ultimately seek the same thing: joy. I'm sure this will prompt you to wonder, 'So then, what exactly are they fighting over?' It is natural for such a question to cross your mind, and it is my forte to answer such questions. So, in this regard, you must note that the root of the conflict lies in how each defines the 'source of happiness' i.e. 'what brings happiness'. This means that while the

From intuition to sensing frequencies, everything is the result of the harmonious interplay between Nature's mind and the spontaneous mind

commands of both these forces are aimed at achieving happiness, both hold contradictory views about the 'methods' to achieve it. Grasp each word carefully, because here, I am once again revealing the profound science about your inner system. This will not only help you recognise your inner system, but also relieve you of all confusions arising due to the conflict between the mind and brain-ego.

At present, grasp well that the brain is extroverted, seeking happiness from external sources, while the mind is introverted, finding joy within. And this is the prime reason behind the conflict between these two entities. Furthermore, while both the brain and mind can form desires, they cannot act on them directly. It is the 'body' that executes the commands arising from these desires. In the example stated earlier, the horse's masters may wish to ride in different directions, but they are dependent on the horse to take them in the desired direction.

In short, the mind and brain-ego compel the body to race in the direction they desire. But since there is only one body, it cannot simultaneously follow conflicting commands, thus creating confusion about whom to obey. And this confusion leads to a pause in action, and naturally, a pause on deeds brings life as well as progress to a grinding halt. This is because life is driven solely by deeds, and progress too is impossible without performing deeds.

In essence, life comes to a standstill time and again, caught in the conflict between the mind and brain-ego. The flow of life is disrupted, because this is a struggle that never ends! Honestly, a large chunk of everyone's time and energy is wasted in this confusion alone, as caught in its web, they are neither able to perform deeds nor choose a direction in life. They take two steps in one direction and two in another. Hence, I request you, don't ever take the confusion stemming from the 'conflict between the mind and brain-ego' lightly.

Fortunately, we have identified the cause underlying this confusion and recognised the importance of eliminating it from our lives. But how do we go about it? To begin, we need to grasp the intricacies of the conflict between these two forces. We will have to delve into their differing desires, for as mentioned earlier, both the brain and the mind are immensely influential. I've also explained that the brain is 'extroverted,' while the mind is 'introverted'. And since both forces are active in everyone, each person is an extrovert in some aspects of life and an introvert in others. The only difference is that those with a stronger brain-ego are more extroverted, while those with a stronger mind lean more towards introversion.

What we need to recognise is that it is completely natural for an introvert and an extrovert to have different desires. And the most striking difference between their desires is: the brain is more interested in portraying 'happiness' than actually being happy as it is influenced by the ego. Hence, its happiness mainly depends on making others jealous and seeking their admiration, respect and reverence. And naturally, such happiness can be attained only when the body toils, whether it is by working relentlessly to earn money, spending hours at the gym for a perfect body, accumulating status symbols like prestigious academic degrees or material possessions, or adhering to societal and religious standards. Because it is only then that others will be jealous of you and shower praises on you. Chasing after bigger cars, better apartments, higher qualifications or the tag of a nobler and devout person are the sort of desires harboured by the brain-ego, and funnily, there is no end to such desires.

Well, the issue wouldn't be as problematic if the story ended here. If the body simply obeyed the brain-ego's commands, everything might flow smoothly. After all, the brain's desires are aimed at helping you progress in life, bringing you respect and honour. So, such desires cannot be disregarded or labelled completely wrong either. In fact, if this was the only voice within us, life would be much simpler. But as I have pointed out, there is another powerful voice—the mind. And the mind doesn't share the brain's inclination for hard work and effort.

The mind isn't interested in pushing itself to acquire expensive cars or luxurious houses. It's not that the mind doesn't desire material things; it just rejects the idea of enduring hardship to fulfil those desires. For the mind, happiness is found in simpler pleasures such as eating, travelling, spending time with friends, watching TV and enjoying leisurely activities. In fact, the mind would love to earn money too, but only if it can be earned effortlessly. It is interested only in deeds that can be executed with 'concentration and enjoyment'.

In essence, the mind desires everything the world has to offer, but it is unwilling to undergo unnecessary effort to fulfil those desires. Simply put, the mind wants to live for itself—it is focused on happiness, not on exerting itself to prove its happiness to others. It doesn't want to create stress or hardship just to demonstrate how happy it is, nor does it feel compelled to suppress its inner joy for the sake of external pressures, influences, beliefs or traditions. The mind's reasoning is straightforward: if I am overweight, that's how I am; why should I push myself to exercise or follow a strict diet? It would be great to gain respect and honour, but if it doesn't come, I won't jeopardise my inner peace just to get in shape. This shows that the mind's approach is the complete opposite of the brain-ego's, and both these opposing forces live within you. And I'm sure, after my detailed explanation, you must have begun to identify both voices. Since I only speak psychological truths, you can certainly experience everything I have stated within you with a little bit of effort. I don't speak of unfounded ideas or lofty concepts wrapped in sweet-sounding words because the solutions to all problems are invariably hidden in bitter pills of profound 'psychological truths'.

By now, you must have gauged that two extremely powerful and opposing forces co-exist within you. You've probably also noticed that these forces constantly pull you in different directions every day. Consider this awareness a significant psychological milestone. And from this point onwards, observe the conflicting urges that arise from these two forces. While the brain encourages you to work harder to earn more, the mind suggests you relax and watch a movie instead. And this is where confusion creeps in. If the mind decides taking a day off for rest, the ego quickly jumps in and cautions you about the importance of completing certain tasks. The brain pushes you towards success and recognition, while the mind urges you to enjoy life and live to the fullest. And in this ongoing battle, the body is the one that suffers, caught in the middle, unsure of whose command to follow. Given that this is a common occurrence in your life, I'm sure you must have experienced many such dilemmas.

Unfortunately, the story does not end here. If you decide to follow the brain's command and get down to work, the mind begins to interfere. It distracts you from focusing on work and starts to tempt you with other plans. Essentially, if you ignore the mind, it will do everything it can to derail your efforts, making you question why you listened to the brain in the first place. And if you give in to the mind's urge for enjoyment, you will end up regretting it. For, when you heed your mind and engage in fun activities, the ego will remind you of the consequences of neglecting work, warning you that your life will fall apart if you continue to waste time in fun and leisurely activities. The ego cautions you that a laidback attitude will cost you both respect and honour. This implies, you first have to bear the confusion of whether you should listen to your brain or your mind, and even if you overcome this confusion and listen to one of them, the other doesn't stop troubling you afterwards. I'm sure you can relate to these inner conflicts, as they are an everyday experience for you. I, therefore, do not see the need to provide multiple examples to illustrate this point. Observe keenly and you will surely find yourself caught between these two forces several times in a day.

Well, let us now explore the methods to eliminate the confusion arising from the conflict between the two, and in that regard, let me first make it clear that Nature has already provided a solution for managing the conflicts between the mind, brain, ego and senses. In fact, Nature has given intelligence to man solely to help him maintain a perfect harmony between these four forces. Intelligence means the ability to make decisions, whether they are related to the conflict between these four forces or any other aspect of life. It is the role of intelligence to guide us in making the best decision in every situation—and yes, this intelligence is often referred to as inner sense.

For now, it is clear that it is up to our intelligence to ensure we aren't caught in the clash of the 'contradictory desires' of the four forces. The first step, then, is to learn how to strike a balance between these forces using our intelligence. And in that context, it is important to understand that none of these forces can be considered inferior or insignificant. Each one must be acknowledged and respected because none of them is an 'enemy' to your life. All four forces ultimately want your happiness. The senses want to infuse life with enjoyment, arousing interest in sensory pleasures like delicious tastes and pleasant aromas. The mind is inherently a seeker of happiness, and in today's world, we definitely need money to sustain ourselves, and to that end, the brain-ego inspire us to earn a livelihood. While the mind and senses may have endless desires, these can only be fulfilled on the strength of the brain-ego. Thus, all four forces are essential to live life to the fullest.

Of course, all four have their own flaws, but that doesn't diminish their worth or usefulness. Therefore, simply ignore the teachings that advocate restraining or suppressing any of these forces. Those who lack an understanding of human psychology continue to criticise and condemn the urges of the mind, ego and senses, so don't waste time arguing with them; simply avoid

> **It does not take long for gains to turn into losses, and losses into gains**

them. Comprehend well that these four forces are the foundational pillars of your life, helping you sustain your life. If they have flaws, so be it. We've been granted intelligence to protect ourselves from their negative effects. Honestly, those who criticise the urges of these forces lack the intelligence to 'tackle' them. To cite an example, a wise and supremely intelligent being like Krishna says to Arjuna in a frank and direct manner, "O Arjuna, know me to be everything, be it lust, anger or ego." So, don't consider any of these forces your enemy despite what teachings imparted by fearful people may say.

To sum it up, all four forces are beneficial because they help us move forward in life. The real challenge is not conquering them, but triumphing over the conflicts that arise between them. We don't need to repress or control them; we simply need to learn to manage them. Moreover, Nature has already made arrangements to rein them in; you just need to act in accordance with that arrangement. Understand that Nature has given us 24 hours in a day, divided into three periods of eight hours each. Each period is dedicated to specific 'deeds', and each period has its own 'master'. The first eight hours are dedicated to earning a livelihood, and in this period, the brain and ego should take charge. If the mind and senses try to distract you from work, remind them, "If I don't focus on my work, none of your desires will be fulfilled." Indeed, it is essential to earn money to satisfy the desires of the mind and ego, and money can only be earned by sincerely engaging in work.

To summarise, you must rein in the flights of your mind and senses as much as possible while you're working. Convince them to

'True spirituality' is simply surrendering your worries to Nature

cooperate so that you can focus, because you will never be able to concentrate on work unless your mind too is engaged alongside your brain and ego. Indeed, a distracted mind will lead you astray by diverting your attention towards numerous other things, but you must not be swayed by it. During the eight hours of work, your brain and ego must hold full authority, but yes, secure the cooperation of the mind with the help of your intelligence, as it is crucial for the mind to be fully engaged in work. In essence, the brain and ego are the only masters during the eight hours of work, so you must obey only their commands. But at the same time, the mind's cooperation is essential, for without its full engagement, any deed that is performed will ultimately be rendered useless. In short, the brain-ego and mind must work in harmony.

Once the mind has cooperated with the brain-ego for eight hours of focused work, it is important to reward it by giving it the command of the next eight hours. During this time, avoid bringing the stress of work with you. Allow the mind to indulge in activities that bring pleasure—watch a movie, spend time with your loved ones, or engage in other enjoyable pursuits. In essence, let the mind be in full control during these eight hours. Once you ensure the mind is content, it will naturally support the brain-ego the following day as well. For, it will be assured that by supporting the brain-ego, it will receive due care and attention and its wishes will be fulfilled. So, it is crucial to take care of the mind for these eight hours as only then will it allow you to work peacefully and productively the next day. This is why, as crucial as it is to work, it is equally important to take a 'break'. And the more refreshing and fulfilling the break, the more effective and focused your work will be. I am sharing profound principles here, so take full advantage of them. Now, let's look at the third eight-hour segment. Allocate this period of time to satiate your senses. Gratify them with your favourite foods, ensure they get the rest they need, and allow yourself a good night's sleep. A little effort here will surely put an end to the conflicts between the mind, brain-ego and senses, helping eliminate any confusion created by their conflicts.

Of course, life has its ups and downs and things don't always go according to plan. Time and circumstances do not remain the same, so you'll need to be flexible with how you divide your day. If you have urgent work that demands more time, reduce the mind's eight hours and give that time to the brain-ego. If the mind feels drained, cut back on work for a few hours to allow the mind extra time to enjoy itself. If the body is tired, dedicate a day to satisfy the senses. Use your intelligence to adjust your schedule as needed, sometimes as per the demands of life and at other times based on your inner needs. This way, you can avoid being caught in the conflict between these four forces and overcome a major cause of confusion. However, keep in mind that this division of the day into three eight-hour segments is a general guideline. You don't need to obsess over the clock. In today's world, even the time spent in travelling can be put to good use, whether for work, entertainment or rest. So, consider the eight-hour framework more as a suggestion or guideline.

Now that we have explored this topic, let me acquaint you with yet another fact. All four forces—the mind, brain, ego and senses—are equally significant. If any of them become weak or dissatisfied, some aspect of your life will lose its vibrancy; whereas our goal is to live a rich, multi-dimensional life, similar to Krishna. Our aim is to suffuse our life with vibrant hues. Once again, this is an important point I am making, so pay close attention. Most people fail to strike this balance, and as a result, they turn the melodious song of their life into a discordant tune. But you must not make this mistake. Understand that it is the 'ego' that gives a human being the 'determination' to perform deeds. So, don't disregard the ego as something useless. This is why, in the Bhagavad Gita, Krishna says, "O Arjuna, consider me to be the ego as well." This statement clearly shows that the ego is also a 'form' of Krishna. If you lack determination in your tasks, you won't accomplish anything substantial in life, nor be able to enjoy any task in its entirety. And as for the flaws that exist in the ego, I have already mentioned at the beginning of this discussion that every entity engages in deeds that invariably produce some bad outcome. If even the sun and water—our very life sources—are not exempt from this law, what can we say about the ego?

In a similar manner, comprehend the usefulness of the brain as well. If your brain isn't functioning well, you won't be able to plan effectively or analyse matters in depth. In fact, without its support, you won't be able to complete any task efficiently. In the same way, if you suppress the mind, you'll lose the ability to enjoy or concentrate on your work, leading to frustration and irritability. Likewise, suppressing your senses will lead to health problems and cause you to lose interest in life itself. Therefore, while it is essential for all four forces to be active, it is equally important to give each of them the importance and attention they deserve. Otherwise, you'll end up living a dull and incomplete life. If you observe closely, you'll see that many people lead such lives. For example, some may achieve great career success but have no hobbies or interests. Others may nurse dreams of a grand future but have no tangible accomplishments in their career. Some people allow their senses to dominate them, reducing their existence to mere eating, drinking and sleeping. Such lives are incomplete and you must ensure yours doesn't slip into this imbalance. No matter what, you must nurture all four forces, making optimal 'use' of each one of them and ensuring they are fully 'content'.

In essence, you must live a multifaceted and complete life, just like Krishna. To achieve this, understand that if the

> **Your 'spontaneous mind' is powerful because it is wirelessly connected to Nature**

brain-ego become the masters of the body for sixteen hours instead of eight, the very charm of life will be lost. If the mind takes over for sixteen hours, you will end up living an impoverished existence. And if the senses overpower the other forces, you'll end up living a life of indolence. Hence, it is crucial to maintain harmony among these four forces. Once this balance is achieved, everything else will automatically fall into place. Most importantly, one of the major sources of confusion will be eliminated.

What Will Others Say?

By now, we have understood that confusion halts action, instantly putting the brakes on deeds. Whereas, the fact remains that deeds are the only means to 'live' as well as carve a spectacular life. Indeed, whether you're living life to the fullest—enjoying your favourite foods, travelling to exotic destinations, watching a movie, or indulging in other pleasures, you have to inevitably perform deeds. Similarly, to carve a magnificent life, you must perform deeds, be it going to work, running your business or attending meetings. Every moment of your life and every achievement you pursue requires action. But confusion applies brakes to all these deeds without exception. And a halt on deeds implies performing lesser number of deeds and living half-heartedly with fewer possibilities. Whereas, in the brief time we have on earth, we should ideally strive to accomplish countless deeds and live as fully as possible. And for that purpose, we must free ourselves from confusion at all costs. And this is precisely why we are addressing the causes of confusion, one by one.

Now, let's discuss one of the major causes of confusion, one that has been created by human beings themselves. Since the beginning of time, this cause has been dominating our minds constantly, holding nearly everyone in its grip. The cause I am referring to is—what will people think? If you reflect deeply, you'll realise this thought often dominates your mind as well. In fact, this thought is so pervasive that it is now closely interlinked with almost all the deeds a human being performs. The moment you consider doing something, thoughts of 'what will people say' or 'what will people think' pop up. Yes, I am speaking of the man living on this very earth! Yes, I am talking about you, so kindly introspect. You'll see that this thought has become automatically connected with everything you do. No matter the deed, as soon as you think of performing it, your mind fills up with worries about what others might think. And this is far more dangerous than you may realise. When the thought of "what will people think?" grips your mind before every action, it forces you to first pause and contemplate it. And in order to contemplate, you need to put your intended action on hold. Now, just think, if you keep delaying your actions this way, when will you ever act? How will you accomplish anything? So, take a moment to reflect on this insight. Engage in deep introspection and you'll discover the truth in these words. And this introspection is crucial because you must first recognise that you are suffering from an 'illness' before seeking treatment. If you are not aware that you're suffering from an illness, how can you treat it?

Well, coming back to the affliction called 'what will people think?', it has overpowered your mind to such an extent that you don't even need to dig deep to uncover it. A simple observation of your daily actions will reveal it. Surely, you will notice countless examples of it in your life, because the list of "people" whose opinions you're concerned about is extensive—from family, friends and belief systems to traditions, religions and society as a whole. For instance, you might think, "I really want to do this, but what

Human life, lived with grace and splendour, can make even Nature envy its magnificence

will my father think?" or "I should do this, but what will the world say?" You may even face conflicts like "I'm hungry, but my beliefs say I should fast," or "I want to do this, but my traditions forbid it." Maybe it is thoughts like, "This activity is enjoyable, but I'm worried my wife won't like it," or "I don't feel like waking up early, but I must go to the temple because of religious customs." If you simply observe yourself for a day, you'll see multiple instances of this. Unfortunately, you have no clue how harmful this mindset is to your life.

Well, I have strongly hinted at this and I'm sure many of you must have grasped it as well. Still, I will break it down in detail, step by step. First, let me ask: Who are you? Obviously, a human being. But what is a human being essentially? A human being is the only creature in Nature endowed with the 'intelligence' to determine 'what actions to take'. This is why only human beings have the freedom to perform a myriad of deeds—a privilege that no other species shares. The sun, for example, cannot choose to flow like water, even if it desires so. Water cannot stand still like the mountains, no matter how much it might wish to. Plants and animals also do not enjoy extensive freedom. In essence, except for the human being, the actions of all others are governed and controlled by 'Nature'. Even animals must live within certain predetermined parameters, because they lack the 'intelligence' to make decisions. And since they do not have this 'intelligence', Nature has maintained its governance and control over them. But you ought to comprehend that you are a human being and Nature has equipped you with immeasurable 'intelligence'. In fact, it trusts you to the extent that it is not controlling your actions even a wee bit. Given this, just think, what will happen if you fail to use your intelligence? So, kindly do not squander this opportunity. Nature has given you the freedom and placed its trust in you, so live up to that trust. Pursue whatever you wish and become whoever you choose to be. Just make sure you use your intelligence in everything you do and in all your pursuits and endeavours. I don't think I can make this point any clearer than I have. However, remember, while you have freedom, you must also respect the laws of Nature while performing any deed. This bit of 'control' is necessary too—after all, there should be some difference between Nature and a human being! I have revealed to you the ultimate secret of Nature, so grasp it in its entirety. Don't let the profound psychoanalysis of 'what will people think' discussed above go in vain.

To sum it up, you are a human being, and Nature has given you the intelligence to determine which actions you should take and which ones you should avoid. And everyone possesses this intelligence in equal measure; Nature is not biased in any way. However, if someone does not want to use their intelligence, that is their personal choice. If they don't trust their intelligence, that is their fault. But you must understand that Nature has granted you complete freedom only because it has full faith in your intelligence. So, when thoughts like "What will people think?" or "What have they said?" pop into your mind, what does it reveal? It shows that at present, you don't fully trust your intelligence. This is yet another simple psychological truth that I have shared with you. Tell me, is it good to doubt your intelligence? In fact, there's nothing worse than this! A human being is a storehouse of intelligence, and if such a reservoir of intelligence believes that he does not possess even the intelligence to determine which actions he must perform or avoid, then this is truly deplorable! I always speak from the ultimate height of spirituality and psychology, so pay serious attention to everything I state. It is indeed dangerous to believe that you lack intelligence. To think so is to acknowledge that you still lack the qualities of an intelligent being. This also implies that at every step, you will have to be instructed regarding the actions you must perform or avoid. And truly, if you don't trust your own intelligence, what a tragedy it is to be born human! Nature had placed great hope in you when sending you into this world, but you have not only dashed your own hopes, but also Nature's.

Well, I am proceeding with this discussion assuming you have grasped the strong indication I have given. If yes, then the first step is to awaken the confidence within yourself that you are an intelligent human being. Honestly, a person without intelligence cannot be called human, for the very identity of a human being is his 'intelligence'. So, believe me when I say this: You are intelligent. From now on, don't let any doubts cloud this truth. The key point to understand is that your intelligence hasn't diminished completely. You have certainly made countless decisions in your life without deliberating over what others might think, and you have executed all those deeds without confusion. So, I find it strange—if you can use your intelligence to execute a few deeds, why not perform all your deeds the same way? You must, for only then will you be able to break free from the shackles of confusion. Otherwise, you'll be stuck in a constant conflict between your desires and the opinions of others, leaving you unable to take action and letting life slip by pointlessly.

It is interesting how the notion of "What will people think?" can arise even when you're pursuing innocent joys or simple, harmless hobbies. You seek happiness through various avenues, and there is no doubt you have the ability to achieve many things, but as soon as the thought of 'what others might think' enters your mind, everything comes to a grinding halt. Remember, life is a rare opportunity to suffuse yourself with happiness, a chance you won't get again. Yet, you allow yourself to miss out on countless beautiful opportunities by thinking about others' opinions. This is foolishness at its peak! The people whose opinions you're so worried about aren't taking care of you, and you're not deriving any happiness

Every human being is 'naturally capable' of leading a great life

from them. Despite this, you are throttling your happiness and burying thousands of your wishes for the sake of their opinions! In doing so, you are either delaying or entirely abandoning the actions that bring you happiness. By suppressing your desires, you are dying a slow death within, falling prey to irritability, frustration and even illnesses. But now, stop putting yourself through this suffering! End this clash between two contradictory desires. You are a human being, and Nature has given you intelligence. You must, therefore, carve a grand life and also live wholeheartedly on the strength of that intelligence. But how will it help if you allow someone else's intelligence to influence you? What others think is rooted in their intelligence, and since you have your own, why borrow theirs?

In essence, there is no denying the fact that you possess intelligence. Only you can determine what is or isn't beneficial for you. So, the first step is to awaken the confidence in yourself that you are an intelligent human being. At the very least, start making decisions by yourself. I'm not suggesting that you completely disregard the thoughts and ideas of others. There is nothing wrong in listening to good advice. However, the opinions of others cannot dictate what you must or must not do. You need to make your own decisions. If you believe your desires are more important than the opinions of others, then prioritise fulfilling your desires. Never allow the pressure of others' opinions to interfere with your decision-making. Realise this—no one can understand your life, your deeds or your happiness better than you do. And when I say no one, I truly mean no one. There are no exceptions in the realm of spirituality. Even those you worship cannot know your path to happiness better than you. This is the design of Nature, and you will have to respect this design.

In short, your intelligence is the closest and most trustworthy guide you have. Nature has endowed everyone with the same amount of intelligence, with no partiality whatsoever. Of course, if someone fails to utilise their intelligence or mistrusts it, then that's a different matter. Here's a simple spiritual principle to grasp: People who rely on borrowed intelligence can never truly connect with Nature. Because it is only the 'individual intelligence' of every person that can connect with Nature. However, in their attempts to accumulate borrowed intelligence, everyone ends up severing their own connection with Nature. This is a deep truth I'm sharing with you, and it will help you understand why people who refer to scriptures day and night are not able to connect with Nature—it is because they are living on borrowed intelligence.

For now, understand well that the opinions and thoughts of others represent borrowed intelligence. And borrowed intelligence inevitably leads to a clash between your intelligence and that of others, based on their opinions. And when two types of intelligence collide, confusion ensues. In other words, your actions will be put on hold, you'll feel trapped, your mind will become restless, and fear will creep in—all because you lack trust in your own intelligence. The sad truth is that, for many, up to eighty percent of life's decisions are being shaped by the thoughts and opinions of others. It saddens me to say that this is what we call 'human life'!

Let me ask you: Do you believe Nature has discriminated against you? Do you think it has given you less intelligence than others? Please don't insult Nature by replying in the affirmative. Deep down, you know this is not true. The key is having faith in your intelligence. Once it is awakened, you will learn to use your intelligence. True spiritual teachings are aimed at awakening your intelligence. They never ask you to perform certain actions or avoid others—such nonsense is propagated by religion and society. Spirituality recognises the fact that you are 'intelligent' and no one knows you better than you know yourself. That is why it focuses on awakening your intelligence so that you can perform your deeds without confusion and live wholeheartedly too. So, if you wish to rid yourself of confusion and live life to the fullest, seek refuge in true spiritual teachings. Unfortunately, the so-called religion and society have collectively perplexed everyone. They neither understand the design of Nature nor the inner framework of the human being, and as a result, they hand out endless lists of dos and don'ts, dictating which actions you should take and which you should avoid. And by blindly following these lists, you weaken your own intelligence. But this isn't the end of it. This problem has dug its roots in everyone—from your family to your friends. While religion and society have dimmed everyone's intelligence by handing out elaborate lists, friends and family have ruined the life of their dear ones by being judgmental. The pressure of "What will people think?" has become so overwhelming, it's beyond words! This is the reason why I had stated at the outset of this topic that 'what people will think' has now become directly interlinked with everyone's deeds. The moment you consider doing something, the thought of others' opinions creeps in, leading to confusion. And as a result, you hesitate and put the deed on hold.

Frankly speaking, "What will people think?" has become so problematic, it could easily be considered one of humanity's greatest burdens. This single notion has given rise to a multitude of problems—an overwhelming sense of confusion, a pause on deeds, a dull and boring life, a weary and depressed mind and many other inexplicable struggles. Truth be told, this thought has shackled the free-spirited mind. And my goal is to help you break free from the debilitating mindset of "What will people think?" Believe me, once you free yourself from this ailment, everything you desire in life will be within your reach. I will, of course, explain everything you need to know, but it is up to you to sharpen your intelligence and

Everything that unfolds in a human being's life is either because of 'Nature' or the 'human being' himself

summon the courage to apply it in your life. If you let this chance slip away, your life will be spent in suppressing yourself, overwhelmed by external pressures and trapped in confusion. This is because everything I state is rooted in the deepest principles of psycho-spirituality, and I express these truths in the simplest terms to make them accessible. But if my words fail to transform you, then all will be lost. So, I urge you to absorb my explanations in their entirety. To make it easier, I will summarise the key points from the above discussion. My aim is to free your mind from the confusion caused by the thought 'what will people think', to multiply the joy in your life, and to accelerate the pace of your deeds. My only expectation is that you grasp these 'profound matters' in their entirety. Opportunities like this, to learn the profound secrets of life and Nature, do not come easily. Therefore, I need not emphasise to someone as intelligent as you the importance of seizing this opportunity. Now, to help you grasp the crux of this matter, here are some key pointers. But remember, it takes both understanding and action to make the most of them.

1. Among all species, human beings are the only ones who have been granted complete freedom by Nature to perform deeds. The reason Nature places such unwavering trust in man is because it has endowed him with intelligence. And since Nature is impartial, this intelligence is bestowed equally upon all individuals, without exception.

2. With intelligence fully available to everyone, no one needs to rely on borrowed intelligence to determine 'which actions to perform or avoid'. Although borrowed intelligence can give an indication, the final decision must rest with the individual himself. This is crucial, because only someone who trusts and acts based on his own intelligence can stay connected with Nature. And if you want to make great strides in life and live majestically, staying connected with Nature is essential.

3. If Nature has granted everyone intelligence, it is obviously meant to be used. Had the intention been for people to live off borrowed intelligence, Nature would have only given this gift to a select few. And had that been the case, there might be reason to worry about the opinions of others. But since that is not the case, why should you concern yourself with others' opinions? Just as your hunger isn't satiated by someone else consuming food, how can you carve a magnificent life relying on the intelligence of others? It truly baffles me why you act against the arrangement of Nature!

4. Everyone knows they possess a mind as well as intelligence. They can even sense the desires of their mind and interpret the signals from their intelligence about which actions to take or avoid. So, why does a person still worry about what others might think? The reason is simple: they lack faith in their own 'desires' and 'intelligence'. And even if their faith is restored to some degree, the overwhelming pressure from the outside world often prevents them from summoning the courage to act independently.

5. You must understand that no one becomes a sinner or is condemned to hell simply because someone says so. Similarly, you do not become a bad person because someone labels you as such, nor do you become aberrant or rogue by opposing someone. All of this is nothing but the collective pressure from others, and unfortunately, the weak often fall victim to these tactics. However, you must rise above this as a strong individual. You entered this world with the life you were bestowed with, and you will depart it in the same manner. You are answerable only to your own soul and Nature for how you lived your life. No third party holds a claim over this, nor are you answerable to anyone else. So, why should you unnecessarily bear the weight of "what others think or say"?

6. Buddha was born into a Hindu family, yet he strongly opposed Hindu traditions and customs. He did not concern himself with scriptures or the opinions of others. Had he done so, he would have never become the great Buddha. Similarly, Christ, although of Jewish descent, rejected many Jewish traditions. Had he worried about "what people would think," he would have never become Christ. And what do I say about Krishna! He embraced everything wholeheartedly—when did he ever have the time to worry about trivial concerns such as "what people would think"? Just reflect for a moment: ignoring the wisdom of these great figures, whom are you choosing to follow?

7. In essence, you need to comprehend that you have the intelligence to decide "which actions you must perform or avoid". You are a unique individual, and there is no one in this world who is exactly like you, nor are anyone else's circumstances the same as yours. Therefore, only you can determine what should be done in any given situation. And it is to help you make these decisions yourself that Nature has equipped you with intelligence. And it is a well-established spiritual principle that 'unless you learn to use your intelligence, you will remain trapped in confusion'. Indeed, every spiritual principle is a truth set in stone, but the real question is: do you truly wish to free yourself from confusion?

8. Another important question to consider is: despite desires knocking at his door and intelligence urging him to act, why does a person halt his deeds, worrying about what

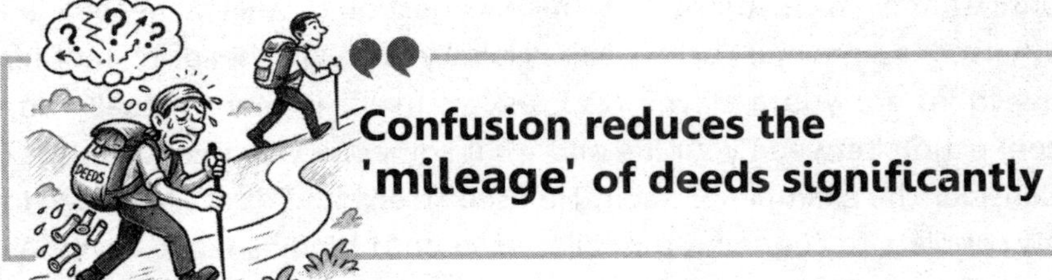

others might think or say? The only logical answer is: he lacks faith in himself. And why is this so? It is because he fears “what if something goes wrong”. But consider this: what’s the guarantee that nothing will go wrong if you live your life relying on others' intelligence? Even now, you are living your life guided by the opinions of others—has that eliminated the problems from your life? All day long, you continue to perform antics guided by the opinions of hundreds of ringmasters, but has that advice helped you create a grand life? Absolutely not! So, why not realise that the fear of “something going wrong” is misplaced to begin with! Moreover, you cannot even hold others responsible when something actually goes wrong. But if you follow your own intelligence, you can hold yourself accountable. When you make mistakes, you can learn from them and eventually, with each lesson, your intelligence will grow sharper, and your trust in it will increase. So, let go of the fear that things will go wrong. The truth is, things can go wrong no matter whose intelligence you follow. However, if you walk the path guided by your own intelligence, you’ll find that the chances of things going wrong are fewer, because no one knows you and your life better than you do.

9. There is another psychological reason behind the concern of "what people will think," and that is the desire to gain others' respect. Naturally, others will respect you only when you act according to their opinions. Whether it is your family, society, religion or authority figures like parents and teachers, you will win their respect only when you conform to their views. If you don't, you may be labelled as a rogue, an outcast or even an atheist. But the real question is, will you become an atheist or a sinner just because they label you so? This leads to another question: are you a slave? Also, ask yourself: is there actually any connection between your life and what someone else thinks or does? Consider the example of Kabir. He used strong and direct language in his couplets to condemn the fallacies in both Hinduism and Islam. As a result, both Hindus and Muslims in Benaras (Varanasi) derided and rebuked him. Yet, despite their scorn, he became the revered "Kabir" that we remember today, whereas those who derided him are simply forgotten. The point is, your life is not defined by others' opinions. You are answerable only to your own soul for the deeds you perform. And when your time comes to leave this world, you will be accountable only to Nature for what you did and how you lived. Let others think what they will and say what they wish. History has always been made by those who lived by their own 'independent intelligence'.

10. Now, let me address one final key point in this discussion. When you move forward in life guided by your own intelligence, then naturally, the entire responsibility for your life will also rest with you—as it should. This is the design of Nature for humanity. In fact, Nature has granted humans freedom so that they can choose whether they want to benefit...or harm themselves. This means they can either use their intelligence for their own good or embody negativity by relying on others' intelligence. Also remember, when we talk about forging ahead on the strength of our own intelligence, we are not referring to following our brain or ego. For example, Kansa relied heavily on his ego and intellect; he too ignored others' opinions, but that doesn't make him intelligent. So, don't mistake the shamelessness, cunningness and reckless abandon of the brain and ego for 'intelligence'. The same goes for Duryodhana who shouldn't be considered an 'intelligent' man either. Compared to him, Arjuna was far better, for although Arjuna lived his entire life depending on others' intelligence, he had at least not enslaved himself to his 'brain-ego'. Thus, if you find that the traits of Kansa or Duryodhana are dominant in you, refrain from using your 'intelligence'. In that case, it would be far better to live your life bound in the clutches of other people's intelligence. In doing so, you will at least not become as outrageous and uncontrolled as Kansa or Duryodhana. Comprehend clearly that this entire knowledge pertaining to 'intelligence' is aimed at those who are like Arjuna. Remember, Krishna had enunciated the Gita specifically to Arjuna. Had it been Duryodhana in Arjuna's place, Krishna would have spoken a different message. Krishna would have expounded to Duryodhana everything that Arjuna was explaining to Krishna in the Gita. And here, I have revealed to you the 'ultimate psychology' of the Gita. Well, for now, comprehend that there are three types of people when it comes to 'intelligence'. The first category comprises individuals like Kansa and Duryodhana who require borrowed intelligence. The second group includes individuals like Arjuna who require the intelligence that I am speaking of at present. The third group is made up of those who are innately intelligent like Krishna. And here, I consider you to be like Arjuna, which is why I am making efforts to awaken your intelligence. But if you are like Kansa or Duryodhana, then neither was the Gita enunciated for your sake nor are my books written with you in mind. In such a scenario, religion and societal rules might be more suitable for you, because it would become necessary to control your brain and ego. Comprehend clearly that religion and society are a prison created specifically for those who start behaving like animals and demons if left unrestrained. And that is precisely why all the teachings of religion and society are aimed at keeping a person on a leash. Freedom can be given to people like 'Arjuna', which is why Krishna sought to awaken his intelligence through the enunciation of Gita. Krishna could very well expound to Arjuna, "Kill everyone, but first awaken your intelligence," but he would never proffer this advice to Duryodhana, because that madman was anyway baying for everyone's blood!

A confused state of mind instantly puts the brakes on deeds

Well, I trust that you have grasped the point I'm hinting at. In fact, this entire topic is intended for those who possess Arjuna's mindset. However, if you fall in the category of individuals like Shakuni, Duryodhana or Kansa, I urge you to continue relying on religious and societal dictates; else, you will stoop down to cruelty and indecency under the garb of 'using your intelligence'. Therefore, let me clarify that I am explaining spiritual psychology to you assuming you to be a normal, intelligent person, and my goal is to awaken that intelligence in its entirety. What is the Bhagavad Gita, after all? It is a scripture to awaken one's intelligence. Throughout the Gita, Krishna was only focused on awakening Arjuna's intelligence. He never stopped Arjuna from asking questions. He never told him to fight the war just because he was asking him to. Krishna's goal was to make Arjuna arrive at the decision to fight based on his own intelligence. This is why Krishna tells him that "Here, a man is his own friend and his own foe. Therefore, he must uplift himself through his own intelligence." And that is exactly what I am trying to explain as well. Nature has given intelligence to you, and those who learn to use it wisely will reap the benefits. The one who neglects this gift will become his own enemy, much like Kansa. Similarly, those who borrow intelligence from individuals like Shakuni will share the same fate as Duryodhana.

To put it simply, your life will become magnificent only on the strength of your own intelligence. So, awaken that intelligence and use it to make all your decisions. Believe me, only then will you be able to live life to its fullest and make your mark in this world. Otherwise, you'll suffocate yourself, trapped in confusion and external pressures. But remember this: while intelligence grants you freedom, it also comes with responsibility. In other words, you alone will become your friend as well as your enemy. Once you choose to heed your own intelligence, you can no longer blame family, society, the world, God or religion for anything. Know with certainty that if someone abides by religious or societal norms, and then blames God, *karma* and its fruits, or astrology, it is only because they are living by those teachings and dictates. But the person who lives by his own intelligence does not have the option of blaming or holding others responsible; in short, he bears full responsibility for his life. As we conclude this discussion, I urge you once again to continue awakening your intelligence and start making decisions in alignment with the wisdom you've gained. Whatever it takes, do it! Don't let my efforts go in vain and no matter what, eliminate the confusion that arises from the notion, "What will others think?"

Know the Size of Your Basket

Let us now explore another key reason behind human confusion. In our discussion so far, I have repeatedly emphasised that ignorance of the 'laws of Nature' is the primary cause of human confusion. The vast majority fails to realise that it is Nature that gives life, and Nature alone has determined 'how to live it'. So, how can we expect to break free from the boundaries that Nature has set for us? Yet, many still try to defy these boundaries and, as a result, fall into confusion. Indeed, if it weren't for our failure to understand and respect the laws of Nature, confusion would not plague our lives.

You must, therefore, always respect Nature's design; disregarding it will only lead to repeated missteps. And to prevent you from falling into these traps, I will now introduce an important aspect of Nature's design. To begin with, you must first recognise that Nature has not made you 'limitless'. You were born with certain limitations set by Nature itself. In other words, Nature first confined you within these limits and then brought you into this world. Sadly, most people are completely unaware of this profound principle—is it any wonder then that life surprises them with constant twists and turns and never-ending challenges! So, embed this truth in your mind: Nature has already 'constrained' you in boundaries and there is no scope for you to violate them.

Given that human beings are bound by limitations, it becomes essential to first understand what those limitations are. Once you grasp this, the rest will become easier to comprehend. But before we dive into the 'limitations of a human being', it is important to reflect on why Nature has sent humans into this world. Why has it arranged such fine provisions like air, water, sunlight and minerals for us? The answer is simple: we are 'Nature's VIP guests'. Nature made these provisions for us long before our arrival to ensure we would not lack the basic necessities—no need to endlessly search for air, water or light. Recognising this fact allows you to appreciate just how invaluable our lives truly are. At the same time, it prompts the question: Why do we fail to appreciate the precious life we've been given? Indeed, if humanity truly valued the gift of life, everyone would take a deeper interest in carving a grand life for themselves by imbibing spiritual and psychological knowledge. I am urging you to build such a life for yourself, so seize this opportunity with both hands!

Now, let's return to our main question: why has Nature made such elaborate arrangements and sent humans into this world as 'VIP guests'? The answer is simple—Nature has done this so that humans could fully experience and enjoy the umpteen offerings this world provides. Therefore, strive to amass everything life has to offer—spirituality, psychology, music, science, literature, wealth! Delight in all the pleasures of life, whether it is fine dining, luxurious clothing, exquisite fragrances or advanced cars and airplanes. Take in the breathtaking beauty of seascapes, tropical forests, snow-capped mountains, gushing waterfalls, and the diverse flora and fauna that adorn our planet. In essence, Nature has sent humans into this world to enjoy and amass everything this world has to offer. Furthermore, it has equipped humans with a 'mind' to make them desire this bounty. Needless to say, all that the 'mind' does is dream up new experiences and pleasures day and night. The mind Nature has bestowed us with is such that it does not want to miss out on any experience of life; it simply wants us to accumulate as much as we can. It has no patience whatsoever! In fact, the mind is designed in such a way that no matter how many joys you indulge in, it will always crave more. This is the nature of the mind we are endowed with, and it is a point worth noting.

Now, you might ask, what's the problem with the mind wanting to experience life's pleasures? Well, the issue is that despite putting in efforts, one fails to satiate the mind, and this leads to confusion, frustration and endless sorrow. But the good news is that you can free yourself from this cycle. Now, I'm sure you're wondering how this is possible. Oh, but how many times must I tell you that you must respect the design of Nature for that purpose! As I've mentioned before, you've been 'confined in limitations' before being sent into this world. So, simply recognise those limitations and accept them. Once you do, you will no longer be overwhelmed by confusion or the problems arising from it. As for the limitations that Nature has confined you in before sending you into this world, I will delve into them in the following pages.

1. The Limitation of Time

Let me ask you a simple question: how long has the Earth been rotating on its axis? How long has the sun been shining in the sky? For how many years have the winds been blowing? These phenomena have been in existence for aeons. The sun has been illuminating the Earth since time immemorial, and the Earth has been rotating for billions of years. Now, tell me—can 'you' claim to have lived for centuries? Of course not! Why? Because you've been sent into this world with a limited time span of around 'hundred years'.

While everything unfolds as per Nature's laws, humans follow their own rules—only to be repeatedly checkmated in the game of life

Everyone knows this or at least they think they do, but the truth is that most people are unaware of its full significance. You may respond by saying, "Don't we know this much?" to which I would assert, "No, you don't!" You'd then probably ask, "Alright, so prove it to us." And I'm eager to do so.

Since you are aware that your life is confined to around hundred years, I'm sure you also understand how many things can realistically be accomplished within that span. So, you must be harbouring desires too within those limits, and even your efforts must be focused only towards the pursuits that can be accomplished within that time span. And if all of this is true, then I can agree that you are indeed aware that the 'basket of your life' comprises only a hundred years. But in reality, this is not the case. It is true that Nature has sent you with a 'basket of a lifespan of hundred years', and ideally, everyone must have a fair idea about the 'limitations of this basket'. Everyone must also know that out of these hundred years, thirty years will inevitably be spent in rest and sleep. So, the actual size of this basket is only about 'seventy years'. This implies, you only have a basket of seventy years to accomplish whatever you wish to. Considering this, it is clear that you cannot become an artist, scientist, painter, writer, doctor, businessperson and anything else you may wish to within this time frame. Note carefully that I'm not referring to the limitations of your intelligence here—I'm only talking about the limitations of time. Even if you have the potential to excel in various fields, there simply isn't enough time to pursue and master them all. Take Einstein, for example. If he did not turn out to be a musician, a spiritual guru as well as a writer, it was because of the limitation of

Nature is neither good nor bad; it is a 'complete balance' of both

time, not because he lacked the potential. Similarly, if a person with a supreme consciousness like Krishna didn't become a scientist or a writer, then the sole reason for this is the finite nature of the 'basket of time'.

Given the limited nature of the 'basket of time', it is clear that you cannot indulge in every hobby or leisure activity, savour every type of cuisine, visit all exotic destinations, or immerse yourself in all art forms. There are over two hundred countries in the world, but because of the constraint of time, it is impossible to explore every corner of each one of them. This means your desires should logically be limited to fit within the scope of a hundred-year lifespan. However, this is not the reality. If you don't believe me, take a moment to list every desire you've had from the moment you were born up to today. Even if you lived for fifty thousand years, fulfilling all those desires would still be an extraordinary achievement! So, how can you honestly claim that you are well aware that your time is limited to a hundred years?

The truth is, your time is limited to a hundred years, yet your list of desires is so extensive that fulfilling them all would take thousands of years. This mismatch is the root cause of the confusion you face every day. Which desire should you prioritise? Which ones should be set aside for the future? And this results in a big mess: you pursue one desire for a while, then chase another for the next couple of days, which means you fail to make 'concentrated effort' towards any of them, and consequently, not a single 'desire' of yours gets fulfilled. And in this process, if something gets 'depleted', it is your basket of time until one day, death knocks at your door and you're left staring at an empty basket. All of this happens because you fail to realise that you possess a limited basket of time. You may know this, but knowing alone isn't enough—you must truly understand it.

So, what should you do? Well, once you have grasped the truth that your basket of time is only about a hundred years, carefully select the desires you can realistically achieve in that timeframe and delete the rest. When you do this, you will be able to apply concentrated effort on the selected desires. And with desires now corresponding to the size of the basket, there will be no room for confusion. This also means that nothing will obstruct the flow of your deeds. In this manner, almost all your selected desires can be fulfilled, and most importantly, you will leave this world with a "basket full of fulfilled desires". But if you fail to implement this learning despite such a clear and simple explanation, you will remain mired in confusion, and your basket of life will also remain empty.

2. The Limitations of Your Body

I need not re-emphasise that Nature has sent you into this world with a limited basket of resources, and the size of this basket determines how many eggs can fit inside. If you try to fill it with more than it can hold, it will inevitably lead to confusion. Indeed, you won't be able to choose one direction determinedly and consequently, you will fail to 'achieve' anything significant in life. Moreover, if you continue to fill your basket indiscriminately, you will crowd it up. You will find that the non-essential 'eggs' have taken up all the space, leaving no room for the essential ones. Take a close look around and you'll see this happening in almost everyone's lives. To avoid this, remember that you have been sent into this world with finite resources—and your body and energy are no exceptions to it. You may aspire to reach the moon and the stars, but the ground reality is that at present, you cannot walk determinedly even on solid ground, let alone reach the stars. So, never forget that your body and energy have their limitations. It is, therefore, better to squeeze in your 'desires' within those limitations; otherwise it is a case of dreaming of climbing mountains but not being able to even step out of bed. Frankly speaking, many people who consider themselves clever and brilliant fall into this trap, but you must not think like them. Use your common sense to adjust your desires within the limitations of your body and energy so that you can at least put in 'concentrated effort' towards fulfilling them. Once you do this, you will begin to fill your basket with the right things. After all, the very purpose of life is to leave this world with a full, blooming basket.

3. The Limitation of Money

It is true that the world is teeming with a variety of offerings that one could acquire, but ultimately, you can acquire only that which can be bought with the money you possess. Therefore, it is crucial to keep your desires within the bounds of the money available at your disposal. This is especially important because most people find themselves in a situation where they have a hundred rupees in hand, yet dream of buying things worth thousands of rupees. This leads to confusing thoughts such as, "Should I get this or that?" "Which of these should I buy?" Caught in confusion, they end up accumulating trash in their basket, while the poor basket sits in anticipation of things you genuinely require. So, stop engaging in such antics! Refrain from falling into confusion or nursing regrets and instead, focus on aligning your desires with the money available to you.

4. The Limitation of Your 'Nature'

In this context, 'nature' refers to a person's disposition. Every individual in this world is born with a 'limited basket of their nature' too, granted by Nature itself. This is why everyone's nature or disposition has certain limitations as well. This is the reason why Buddha cannot do what Krishna can, nor can Christ do what Meera can. Similarly, what Einstein can accomplish, Vivekanand

> **Humans are caught in a vicious cycle—they lament when they perform a deed and regret when they avoid it**

cannot. And yet, here you are—not even aware of 'the limitations of your own nature'. You often think, “Let me tackle this issue and handle that situation,” “Let me teach this person a lesson and set that person straight,” “Let me pursue this field of interest and let me make a mark in that field as well.” Doesn’t all this sound familiar? Consequently, you find yourself swirling in a sea of confusion, accomplishing nothing of significance, and instead spend your life enduring frustration and sorrow. But why must you engage in such pursuits? Take a moment to reflect and write down the limitations of your nature and restrict your desires within those limitations. Recognise that you can only do what your nature allows. So, why invite confusion by taking flights that are beyond the boundaries of your nature?

In essence, Nature has sent every person with a limited set of resources. You may wonder why this is the case. Well, it is because man is not a ‘permanent resident’ of this universe, like the sun, air or earth. Humans are creatures sent on Earth on a "tourist visa" that lasts only a few decades. This is why he has been granted a limited basket of resources. I have outlined four primary “baskets” of your life, but there are many others like these that you must reflect on as well. I have already pointed you in that direction, so it should not be a difficult task for intelligent people like you to identify all other baskets and recognise their limitations.

The key point is: you have arrived in this world with a limited set of resources on a 'tourist visa of hundred years'. So, it would be wise to stay within those boundaries and behave like a tourist. You will not be granted permanent residence in this universe, but despite knowing this, you refuse to accept this reality. You nurse desires that far exceed the size of your basket, and this is a major reason behind all your predicaments. A few ‘intelligent’ individuals might argue that this is actually Nature’s fault, for why did it endow humans with a ‘mind’ that was designed to dream beyond their basket’s capacity. If you’re thinking on these lines, let me tell you that you are failing to fathom the 'mystery of life' itself. Ask yourself: if the mind was unable to indulge in flights of fancy, would there be any fun in living? If the mind was built to fit the size of the basket, life would become dull and drab, devoid of vibrancy! It would become monotonous, much like how animals live their lives. In case you haven't realised it yet, animals have a mind that aligns with the size of their respective baskets, which is why they live free from confusion, strife and sorrow. So, my dear, I object! Don't you ever point a finger at Nature! Instead, be grateful that you are not born into this world as a four-legged animal with a limited mind!

Well, let us concede that Nature must have had its reasons for everything, and that it designed everything after due consideration. But the question remains: Why did Nature give humans a mind capable of soaring high on flights of fancy? Well, in that regard, understand that it has also given them 'intelligence' to rein in those flights, hasn't it? So, can you really blame Nature if you fail to recognise the balance it has established? Understand clearly that Nature has sent you in this world to play a 'video game' in which 'unlimited things' are available to satiate all kinds of desires. To wish for all these unlimited things, it has given every person a 'mind that takes flights of fancy', but at the same time, it has provided a very small 'basket' to collect these things. And to help you fit your desires within the constraints of your small basket and accumulate the choicest and best items from this world, Nature has given you 'intelligence'. 'Intelligence' can also be called consciousness, wisdom or whatever term you prefer. After all, there are many 'word enthusiasts' in this world and they can certainly argue over trivial matters such as Krishna spoke about 'consciousness', never about 'intelligence'. Well, Krishna, for that matter, had never mentioned flying in airplanes either. Really, there are such brilliant people in the world that I am indeed rendered speechless! They are quite likely to ask questions such as, "Why did you use Urdu words while discussing Krishna?" "Why don't you speak only in Sanskrit?" "Why don't you enrol your children to a Sanskrit school?" Honestly, such over smart people exhibiting such utter foolishness could easily win a 'Nobel Prize' for their misguided brilliance!

But my message is simple: don't get caught up in over smartness or the illusion of words. Focus on the essence. And the essence of what I'm saying is this: Nature has designed a 'video game similar to a marketplace' brimming with a variety of offerings. We, as temporary visitors with a 'tourist visa' lasting roughly a hundred years, have one job: to win the game. To win, we must use our intelligence to align our soaring mind with the size of our basket and collect the best possible items from the world. In other words, if you leave this world with your basket full—having chosen wisely and fulfilled your desires—you have won the game. But if you leave with an empty basket, you have lost. And should you depart with nothing of value, Nature will definitely call you into 'remand'. Those who wander aimlessly in the wilderness or the Himalayas or engage in absurd rituals pointlessly are repeatedly summoned in Nature's 'remand house', for they have died with an empty basket. They have missed out on experiencing the wonders of art, the mysteries of science...with many even failing to earn a living for themselves. They have neither tasted the sweet nectar of love nor experienced the joy of familial relationships. Truth be told, they have not made the slightest effort to pick even one egg and put it in their 'basket'. In Nature's remand house, they are asked just one question: 'Why didn't you switch the game on?' So, forget about such people. My concern is you. If you too leave this world with an empty basket due to indecision and confusion, you will face the same fate. Therefore, ensure that when you depart, your basket is filled with accomplished desires. To achieve this, you must apply concentrated effort, and that is only possible if you use your intelligence to align your soaring mind with the limitation of your basket. I am confident that after this in-depth explanation, you will make the necessary efforts.

Why
Do We Act Confused?

So far, we have identified the five main causes of confusion, which broadly speaking, account for about 80 percent of confusion in human lives. In a way, we have uncovered the root cause of confusion. So, let us now explore what constitutes 'confusing behaviour'.

First, it is important to distinguish between 'confusion' and 'confusing behaviour'. When you're confused, you typically put a pause on your deeds so that you can deliberate on them. You assess the situation, make calculations, seek advice or simply try to understand what should be done. In short, when you are gripped with confusion, you are engaged in everything except performing the 'deed'. However, confusing behaviour is different. With confusing behaviour, you continue to perform your deeds, but you take a few steps in one direction and then suddenly change course. You don't stick to one direction. This means you continue to walk, but due to confusion, you are unable to walk determinedly on one path. And such confusing behaviour is no less dangerous than confusion itself. In fact, it is even more dangerous, because due to the ongoing continuity of the deed, your 'time and energy' both are wasted, and yet, you are unable to accomplish anything. The math is simple: one cannot take two steps to the right and then two to the left without wasting time and energy. Besides, it is impossible to reach one's destination in a state of indecision. That is why I state that this is a far greater loss. When you halt a deed due to confusion, you at least don't end up wasting your precious time and energy. However, in confusing behaviour, not only is your time and energy expended, but you are still not able to achieve anything of consequence.

Considering the perils of confusing behaviour, it is important to conduct its complete psychoanalysis. To begin with, grasp clearly that not all aspects of your life result in confusing behaviour. When dealing with objects, for example, your behaviour is always consistent. You don't use a table to sometimes sleep, and other times, to partake of meals. In other words, its use is 100 percent clear to you. Similarly, you use an air conditioner only when you want to cool a room. You don't use an air conditioner to heat the room one day, and use it to cool the next day. This means there is a consistency in your behaviour when dealing with objects, which is why you are able to use them as you wish and benefit from them too.

Now, let's assess your behaviour with respect to human beings. You might love someone today and despise them tomorrow. You may trust a person one moment and doubt them the next. One day, you want to spend a lifetime with someone, and the next, you decide to part ways. There have also been times when you've wanted a person to leave the room, someone whose very presence had once made you happy. Due to all these shifts in your behaviour, neither are you able to strengthen your relationships with anyone nor experience feelings of deep love towards anyone. This is because confusing behaviour can never provide 'stability to relationships'.

In life, it is not always a choice between two good deeds

Truth be told, confusing behaviour creates misconceptions and doubts about you in other people's minds, due to which the other person's behaviour towards you becomes confusing as well. He then starts viewing you as a friend one moment and a stranger the next. In fact, due to these very reasons, your interpersonal relationships do not become as strong and worthwhile as they should. Otherwise, there is no greater source of happiness in the world than the joy found in meaningful relationships. But your confusing behaviour deprives you of this wonderful opportunity to experience happiness.

Another point worth reflecting on is the effort you put into building and maintaining relationships. You invest time, energy and even money into your connections. Yet, because of your confusing behaviour, all your efforts go in vain. This is a significant loss indeed! You ought to realise that the biggest ally of a human being is another 'human being'. Be it happiness and sorrow or the highs and lows of life, we share these with one another. Whether in moments of sorrow or the good times, one yearns the company of fellow human beings on every occasion. This is the reason why people strive to build relationships, but due to 'confusing behaviour', all efforts go down the drain. For example, due to your confusing behaviour, you end up creating a mess in the very organisation you've dedicated years to. This is why I emphasise that you don't realise how costly your confusing behaviour is. But from this moment onwards, pay close attention. Reflect on the fact that despite having several relationships in your life, how many people can you truly count on to share your joys and sorrows? Seriously probe all your relationships at least once and check whether you really have someone in your life who will truly understand and support you. Remember, strong relationships help you weather life's ups and downs. You can deal with all the inadequacies of life, be it financial, health-related or emotional, as long as you have a few cherished relationships. And I'm sure you are aware of all this. That is why you put in tireless efforts to build and maintain your relationships. But when your behaviour is confusing, all your efforts go in vain. Despite nurturing one's relationships with love, care and attention, one is unable to find 'stability' in them. This in itself should give you a clear understanding of how damaging confusing behaviour can be.

Strangely, your confusing behaviour isn't limited to relationships—it also affects your thoughts, ideas and belief systems. Consider the example of one's belief in God. The vast majority believes in God and even practises rites and rituals to please and placate God, but the moot question is, do they truly believe in the existence of God even after engaging in these practices? If they did, they wouldn't perform such deeds...because if God exists, then most certainly, even a leaf isn't quivering without his will! This means that even difficulties are not entering your life without his will. And if this is true, you need not crib and cry in times of adversity. If God exists, he certainly wants the best for you. And since he is looking after your best interests, why worry? Yet, people's behaviour is often confusing when it comes to their faith in God. Their very actions are incongruent with what they proclaim. When they worship God and perform religious rituals, it may seem that they believe in the existence of God, but then these very people also harbour worries, thereby demonstrating that they don't have complete faith in God.

Interestingly, confusing behaviour extends beyond religion and God too, encompassing every notion and idea. There are countless notions that man believes to be noble such as, "Don't spout lies... don't steal... don't ogle at women." But if the opportunity arises or when there is no possibility of him getting caught, he will act against his own thoughts and ideologies, and that too, without blinking an eye! So, the question is: why is your behaviour confusing when it comes to thoughts and opinions? Why does your behaviour change depending on the people you're with or the group or community you're in? Why don't you realise that such confusing behaviour is the reason you are unable to progress in life! You are neither able to digest the fact that God exists nor muster the courage to boldly declare that He doesn't.

In essence, whether it is a thought, belief or God for that matter, you're constantly vacillating—taking two steps in one direction and two steps in another. But what will you achieve ultimately? Comprehend well that if God exists, decisions need to be made in 'a certain way', and if he doesn't, decisions need to be made 'differently'. The same applies to thoughts and opinions. If you nurture thought 'A', you must choose a 'certain path' in life, and if you nurture thought 'B', you must choose a path in life that aligns with that particular thought. However, your behaviour is confusing with respect to every 'thought'. So, no matter how noble your thoughts may be, how will you ever benefit from them? And the most important question is: how will you ever achieve anything significant in life?

To put it simply, your behaviour must be 'steady'. Let me illustrate this point with the examples of a few legendary figures. Buddha was unwavering in his belief that God does not exist. He was so convinced with this notion that he never exhibited confusing behaviour regarding it, which is why he attained enlightenment and became the great Buddha. Krishna, on the other hand, considered the 'soul' to be paramount, so it did not matter to him whether God existed or not. So, he too attained greatness. Similarly, Christ's belief in God was so strong that he showed no confusion in his behaviour. He even embraced crucifixion with a smile, accepting it as a divine blessing. The key point is that no matter what thought or belief you hold, your behaviour must not reflect any confusion regarding it. Only then

Life is shaped by actions, not indecision

will you be able to choose one definite path. And only when you walk determinedly on a single path will you be able to reach your destination.

By now, you must have understood how dangerous confusing behaviour can be. But the crucial question remains: why do so many people exhibit such behaviour when it comes to thoughts and fellow human beings? It's one thing if a smaller section acts this way, but when the vast majority does, it calls for deeper reflection. To grasp the matter in its depth, you must first understand your own composition, as the "secret" behind confusing behaviour lies in your basic composition. Understand well that there are two forces controlling your behaviour: your brain-ego and your mind. The brain-ego is easily swayed by external pressure and influences, adopting 'thoughts and opinions' superficially without fully understanding them. One day, you may form an opinion based on someone's viewpoint, and the next, change it after hearing another perspective. And this behaviour of the brain and ego is not restricted to thoughts and opinions only. They behave similarly while forming opinions regarding 'human beings' too. When someone shows a few pleasing traits, your brain-ego quickly form a positive opinion, but after a few bitter experiences, that opinion shifts just as easily. Introspect on your own behaviours and you'll likely recognise these patterns in yourself. And relating to these instances is essential because it is only then that you will realise that many of your own behaviours are confusing too. Besides, before treating any ailment, it is important to first acknowledge that you are afflicted, right?

In contrast to the brain-ego, the mind does not form opinions without a concrete experience. For example,

Society and scriptures may shout their dictates and cry themselves hoarse but they cannot alter the design of Nature

after hearing the opinions of elders or reading scriptures, the brain-ego might accept the idea of God's existence, but the mind won't accept such a belief until it has 'experienced' it first-hand. The mind never accepts any thought or opinion without having experienced it. Neither does it rush to judge a person as good or bad. In short, the mind forms an opinion only after it is fully convinced about the matter through experience. This creates a disconnect between the brain-ego and the mind, resulting in a conflict over ideas, beliefs and even people. The brain and ego may have faith in God based on the ideas they have imbibed, but the mind wants to experience it directly, and such differing opinions ultimately lead to a conflict between the two regarding 'the existence of God'.

As stated earlier, both the mind and brain-ego are powerful entities, which means that sometimes, it is the brain-ego that controls your behaviour, and at other times, it is the mind. When the brain-ego is in charge, your behaviour will reflect the belief that 'God exists', but when the mind controls your behaviour, you end up contradicting your own thoughts. In such a case, your behaviour reflects the notion that 'God does not exist', simply because the mind never concurs with the brain-ego.

To put it simply, how you would behave in a certain moment is determined by which entity is controlling you at that point in time. Is it the mind or the brain-ego? Well, regardless of the entity, the key point is that the mind and the brain-ego 'internalise and accept thoughts' differently, leading to confusing behaviour. Just see, in the course of a simple discussion, we have uncovered a profound 'psychological truth' about our inner self. It is this very power of psychology that I want to awaken in each one of you.

Now, consider one more point: because the brain-ego form opinions instantaneously, they also tend to change their opinions swiftly. For instance, the brain-ego may perceive godliness in a person after observing a few instances of good behaviour, but the same person can quickly turn into a "devil" if they exhibit one negative behaviour. In contrast, the mind is consistent. It doesn't form an opinion easily, but once it does, it doesn't change it frequently. That is why, whether it is thoughts or people, once the mind embraces it, one's behaviour becomes stable. But the predicament is, in most people, the brain-ego dominate the mind, leading them to be easily influenced and quick to change their stance whenever a new idea comes along. If you belong to this category, beware!

By now, you must have understood why your behaviour is stable when dealing with objects. It is because your mind has accepted them only after experiencing them. For instance, your behaviour is consistent around an air conditioner because your mind has experienced that it cools the room. And when something is validated through experience, there is no scope for confusion. Krishna, Kabir or Christ showed no signs of confusion about the 'existence of God', which is why whatever they experienced reflected in their behaviour unwaveringly. There was not an ounce of confusion in Meera's mind regarding the existence of Krishna, and this clearly reflected in her behaviour throughout her life. Regardless of the countless atrocities meted out to her, her behaviour did not change even once. She stood steadfast in her faith, unlike those who proclaim that 'God exists' but lose their footing at the first sign of adversity. This is why I state that if one professes faith in the existence of God, one's conviction should be as unwavering as Christ's. Even as he was crucified, his belief remained intact. Or like Meera, whose heart burnt with love for Krishna regardless of the atrocities she was subjected to. In all the examples stated above, note that the 'consistency' in behaviour was the result of the experience of the mind. In contrast to this, when thoughts are adopted hastily, driven by the brain-ego, it will always result in confusing behaviour. Yes, you have the freedom to adopt any thought, but you must at least stand 'firm' in your thoughts, and that firmness cannot be attained without experience. At this point, let me be very clear: I'm speaking of firmness, not stubbornness. Firmness in thought comes from experience, and experience never deceives you. Stubbornness, however, comes from the ego, and all the thoughts harboured by the ego are borrowed from others. And it is unwise to cling to the thoughts borrowed from others, because more often than not, they lead you astray. So, it is better to weed out such thoughts. If a person realises that certain thoughts are wrong but still clings on to them, then such behaviour is nothing but 'stubbornness'. Hence, never forget the difference between 'firmness in thoughts' and 'stubbornness towards thoughts'. To prevent further confusion, it is essential to gain clarity about these matters.

By now, you must have surely grasped what confusing behaviour is as well as its underlying causes. You must have also comprehended the consequences of confusing behaviour. Nonetheless, allow me to refresh your memory, for it is only when you are fully aware of the potential losses that you will take these matters seriously. The first and most significant loss is that of direction—because you take two steps forward, then two in another direction, you end up nowhere. Moreover, you end up wasting time and energy, thereby feeling drained in the process. This ultimately saps you of energy to perform even those 'deeds that are worth performing'.

In short, confusing behaviour makes life directionless. For instance, just when it seems that relationships are becoming better, all of a sudden, you find them turning sour. So, understand well that confusing behaviour is no less dangerous than confusion itself. The truth is, there is nothing inherently difficult about creating a magnificent life—it is no rocket science. You've

No issue ends with just one 'mistake', as many more are triggered automatically

been blessed with a fully functioning body, mind, intellect, ego and soul, so the journey of life ought to be splendid. However, you will build a splendid life only when you pick a single path unwaveringly. You will carve a wonderful existence only when you walk ahead determinedly. And you will be able to do all this only when your behaviour is not confusing.

Now, let us understand how to overcome confusing behaviour. On this subject, the wise have clearly said: rather than accumulating a thousand good thoughts, it is far better to have just a few good experiences. Why? Because generally speaking, all thoughts are more or less adopted superficially. This is precisely why, in moments of adversity, they fail you. They don't have the strength to carry someone to the gallows with a smile on his face—like Bhagat Singh did. The fervour of patriotism has to be entrenched in 'experience' to make someone sacrifice their life so bravely and heroically.

So, as a first step, resist the urge to form thoughts in haste. Avoid environments and conversations that hand out thoughts and ideologies to you. What's the use of thoughts—good or bad—if they desert you when you need them the most? Why squander your time and energy on them? Understand this: the brain sits at the top of the body, and thoughts are adopted by the brain. This is why all thoughts remain shallow as they don't reach the depths of the mind. So, try not to get lost in the 'illusion of thoughts'. Similarly, don't form opinions on relationships based on limited and superficial experiences. Don't make haste while forming opinions. Let all your experiences seep into the fiery depths of your mind. Allow everything to be experienced in the deepest recesses of your mind. You see, the mind stretches far deeper, down to your very core, your 'navel', which is why once something is assimilated by the mind, it stays with you for a long time and brings consistency in your thoughts and behaviour. So, instead of adopting thoughts superficially, allow everything to seep in and be experienced in the depths of your mind. For, once you experience something deep within, you will remain firm and convinced about it. Believe me, twenty to thirty experiences are more than enough to build a beautiful life. In fact, ten profound and deeply-felt experiences that have seeped into the very core of your being will prove far more fruitful than a thousand notions you have embraced out of force, influence, attraction, greed or compulsion. Instead of nurturing hundreds of relationships that are superficial, a handful of close-knit relationships will enrich your life far more. So, set boundaries—both in thought and in relationships, rooting them in only true and well-founded experiences. Grasp well that 'experiences' will never betray you, and once you gain these experiences, your behaviour will no longer be confusing.

I hope you have grasped the above-mentioned point. So, steer clear of every thought you have adopted superficially without first-hand experience as soon as possible. Engage only in those areas wherein you have a concrete experience. Then just watch how the majority of your problems dissipate, making your life smooth and seamless. To make this point clearer, I have provided a few practical applications below. Fill in the charts and implement their learnings in your life. You will see an instant reduction in your confusing behaviour, and very soon, a day will dawn when you will be rid of it completely.

Practical Application – A

No.	Write down the thoughts you have adopted without first-hand experience	Write that 'I will forsake them!'
1.	....	....
2.	....	....
3.	....	....

4.	....	....
5.	....	....
6.	....	....
7.	....	....
8.	....	....
9.	....	....
10.	....	....

Note: Let go of the ten main thoughts or notions you have held onto over the years—the ones you have accepted without direct experience. Then, from among those ten, reflect on the few that seem truly essential to your life. Once you have gained real, lived experience of those select few, embrace them again. You will realise that barely two or so out of ten genuinely hold value. If even a couple of them resonate with your personal experience, know that that alone is enough. Understand clearly that every individual's life has its own limited range and to carve a beautiful life, you don't need countless experiences—you just need a handful that fall within your unique range. Newton, Einstein and Edison needed 'scientific experiences' but perhaps you don't require that. Grasp this hint and the rest will follow seamlessly.

So, instead of adopting a thousand thoughts superficially, focus on a few strong experiences that are relevant to your life. That is more than enough to shape a magnificent life. Even the most legendary lives in history are nothing but the essence of a 'few experiences'. I have steered you in the right direction, and you are intelligent enough to grasp the crux of my explanation. Here, you must also keep in mind that only by safeguarding yourself from superficial thoughts will you be able to experience something profound within.

Practical Application – B

As I have mentioned before, all you need to shape a grand existence are twenty to thirty firm experiences on the basis of your thoughts. So, in the chart below, list your ten most firm experiences. By "firm experience", I mean a thought or insight that remains unwavering, no matter the circumstances, and does not result in confusing behaviour. For example, a car helps you reach your destination and this is your firm experience. Even if it breaks down once in a while, your core belief that a car will take you to your destination remains unchanged. That is what qualifies as an 'experience'. Initially, you might find it difficult to list ten experiences, but give it your best. I assure you, the day you cultivate thirty thoughts grounded in your own lived experience, you will find yourself transformed phenomenally.

No.	Write about your firm experiences in detail	Note down the reason for your unshakable faith in those experiences
1.	....	....
2.	....	....

3.	....	....
4.	....	....
5.	....	....
6.	....	....
7.	....	....
8.	....	....
9.	....	....
10.	....	....

Practical Application – C

In life, you must have at least ten relationships that you trust completely. Then, no matter what life brings—joy, sorrow, success or struggle—these bonds must remain strong and unwavering. Indeed, there must be at least ten such relationships wherein you are absolutely sure of support in moments of joy and sorrow and the ups and downs of life. So, in the chart below, take a moment to reflect and write down the names of individuals with whom you share such trustworthy bonds. If you currently have fewer than ten, that's okay—start with that. But do pause and ask yourself: what kind of life have I been living if I haven't built even ten concrete relationships?

Make sure you include only those people whose presence in your life feels truly unshakable. Then, regardless of the highs and lows that creep into those relationships, you are confident that they will never fall apart. The day you find yourself with twenty such relationships, you can be sure your life is moving in the right direction. Because reaching that number is only possible when your own behaviour is no longer confusing. So, comprehend clearly that it is due to your confusing behaviour that you don't have even a few strong relationships.

No.	Jot down the names of people you're confident you share a strong, trustworthy connection with	Write down why you have such unshakable faith in these relationships
1.	....	....
2.	....	....
3.	....	....
4.	....	....
5.	....	....
6.	....	....
7.	....	....
8.	....	....

9.	....	....
10.	....	....

There is one important point you must especially take note of: having twenty solid, trustworthy relationships in life is a good sign, and if you have built more than twenty, that is even more commendable. However, at the very least, you must have two to four relationships rooted in absolute trust. If even that much is lacking, it is time for honest reflection. Ask yourself: do I tend to feel confused in relationships, and in turn, confuse others? For, it is confusing behaviour alone that stops interpersonal relationships from thriving and flourishing.

Let's revisit this entire matter from a fresh perspective. A person's confusing behaviour is as detrimental as his own confused state. But what exactly is confusing behaviour? It is when someone behaves one way at one moment, and in a completely different way at another. And this type of behaviour is quite common whether one is dealing with human beings or thoughts. The most serious consequence of such behaviour is that a person constantly wavers and changes his direction, unable to stick to one path. As a result, he suffers two major setbacks. First, he fails to make progress in any one direction. Second, he creates an atmosphere of confusion, making it difficult for others to trust him. Moreover, he is no longer in a position where he can be trusted, because after all, it is essential to have consistency in one's behaviour. All said and done, everyone is compelled to suffer on account of confusing behaviour.

Focus only on your soul and not the world around you. Otherwise, you will always remain confused

By now, you may have noticed this pattern in your own life as well. You've probably had many experiences where your confusing behaviour has cost you dearly. And as for the reason behind such behaviour, it is nothing but 'forming an opinion without a firm, definitive experience'. But despite this, everyone is in such a hurry to adopt and embrace new thoughts and opinions! Consider this: how did you form the thought that you are a Hindu or a Muslim? The answer is simple: as you were born in a Muslim family, you have adopted the thought that you are a Muslim. However, this reflects a primitive mindset. The point worth considering is that there is no profound experience to support the thought that you are a Muslim, and this eventually gives rise to confusing behaviour. Let's consider another example. Islam forbids alcohol, yet many who identify as Muslim consume alcohol while also going about their lives as Muslims. Such perplexing behaviour is seen across all religions, be it Hinduism, Christianity, Buddhism or others. So, remember, as long as you continue to adopt thoughts hastily, you will keep exhibiting such confusing behaviour.

Now answer this: did you embrace the idea of whether God exists or not through experience or haste? Had you embraced the notion "God exists" based on your experience, you too would have gladly accepted crucifixion in the name of God, just like Christ did. On the other hand, if your belief was firmly rooted in the notion that "God does not exist", you would have fearlessly laid down your life for your motherland, just like Bhagat Singh did. However, neither of the above is easy, because the real question isn't whether God exists or not—it's how deeply rooted your experience is behind that thought. If you have formed your thought through experience, you would sail through on the strength of the notion that 'God exists'—or even the notion that 'God does not exist'—because the significance lies not in the thoughts themselves, but in the experience of those thoughts. This is a profound spiritual truth, so do not let it go in vain. Several great personalities like Christ, Kabir, Meera and Chaitanya have acknowledged and embraced the existence of God. At the same time, many remarkable figures like Buddha and Mullah Nasruddin have denied the existence of God. And then there are those like Krishna and Ashtavakra, who believed only their own selves i.e. their soul to be God. Yet all of them are undeniably great and have performed remarkable deeds too, because the significance lies not in thoughts, but in the 'experience' that gave birth to those thoughts. Now, tell me, could there be a more profound realisation than this? But if you still insist on clinging to 'countless thoughts' with 'zero experience' then the choice is yours.

Essentially, you must learn to rein in the habit of embracing thoughts superficially and forming opinions and views in haste. Just reflect for a moment: Is there any area of life where you haven't formed an opinion already? You have a mental checklist for everything—good and bad, healthy and unhealthy foods, moral and immoral, what must be pursued and what should be avoided. This implies, everyone is living in the chaos ensuing from millions of thoughts, opinions and advice. But why don't you realise that there is no need to adopt these superficial thoughts, especially considering the fact that none of them are firm and unshakable. All these superficial thoughts shatter into fragments at the slightest adversity. So, why entertain thoughts that tend to crumble to pieces? It is precisely these superficial thoughts that make your behaviour confusing, and such behaviour is hampering your progress in life.

So, if you truly wish to overcome confusing behaviour, let go of your habit of forming opinions in haste. Comprehend clearly that a few profound experiences are enough to shape a magnificent life, but you will encounter such experiences only when you burn in the fiery trials of life. So, allow yourself to walk through this fire and only then form your 'thoughts' through the searing experiences. Trust me, when you bring this change in yourself, it will lead to a phenomenal transformation in your life.

Going Against Yourself is Dangerous

We have fathomed the major causes of confusion and also looked into the solutions to eliminate them. We have even examined the causes of confusing behaviour and learnt how to safeguard ourselves from it. Additionally, we have gained clarity about the 'size of our basket'. In short, based on all that we have discussed so far, half your confusions should have already begun to dissipate. But here's the reality: confusion has countless faces born from innumerable sources. Therefore, we must discuss those methods too which can eliminate confusion instantly. To do that, you must first understand why you become confused. It is because you tend to expand everything, be it thoughts, knowledge, desires or anything else. This expansion offers you 'unlimited options' which end up confusing you. And this happens because you end up struggling to choose a single path from among all those countless options. So, what is the way out? The solution lies in determining the 'direction of life', which means if we begin to live for a purpose, confusion will vanish from our lives instantly. This is a profound psychological insight, and to explore it further, we shall delve into how to anchor our lives around a single purpose. Believe me, this is the most effective elixir to instantly reduce 'confusion' from life.

But before we do that, there is something crucial you must realise about yourself. You are a human being, and that in itself means you are extraordinarily powerful. Truly, you can achieve anything—reach the Moon and Mars and even rule over the entire cosmos. You can even engage in marvellous creativity and accomplish extraordinary feats. You have the potential to achieve the impossible because Nature has equipped you with unimaginable power. I have no doubt that you can accomplish anything you desire, but let me caution you here: you cannot 'go against yourself' even if you wish to. Apart from this, you are capable of achieving everything. Here, I have once again unveiled a 'profound secret' of life to you, so etch it in your mind: you can achieve anything you desire, but you cannot go against yourself. And who are you essentially? Well, you may have a great many introductions, but in the context of this discussion, you are 'your desires'. Whether they are ten, fifty or hundred, they are uniquely you. And on reflecting deeply, you will realise that you are nothing but 'your desires'. Just imagine your existence without your desires and you will sense a gaping void within yourself.

Now, whether a person has five desires or fifty, what truly matters is recognising that within this multitude, there exist 'three main desires' that are deeply ingrained in every human being. These desires may be linked to life goals, hobbies, passions, interests or even relationships—or something entirely different, but regardless of that, everyone has three core desires which are their very 'lifeline'.

So, essentially, a human being is a living repository of desires and every individual carries countless wants and wishes—however, not all of them are deep-rooted. The majority of desires are superficial, materialising quickly and even changing frequently. So, let us ignore those desires as they are not central to who we are. What truly matters—and what we will explore here—are the 'three core desires' that are so deeply rooted, they become an inseparable part of a person's identity.

Here, let me clarify that this book isn't about the 'psychology of desires'. However, it is crucial to clarify a few points about desires, the first being, all desires are future-oriented. And the future, by its very nature, is beyond our control. This means that merely wanting something doesn't guarantee its realisation. This also means that when desires remain unfulfilled, one is bound to endure sorrow. Hence, you must never forget that 'desires' are the 'root cause of sorrow'. Also, do not wrongly assume that I am 'promoting or advocating desires', but yes, the desires I am referring to presently are the ones that have become an 'inseparable part of a human being's existence'.

Let's suppose music is an intrinsic part of someone's personality, so how can that person be separated from their passion for it? Agreed, his desires regarding music are tied to the future, but they are still an integral part of his existence, aren't they? This is because his desire to compose music will exist even tomorrow and even after ten years. Think of it this way: the desire to breathe is also ultimately related to the future; but as far as breathing is concerned, it is certain that you wish to breathe forever, because the moment you stop, everything ends. In the same way, the three core desires I speak of are not just desires. Although they pertain to the future, they cannot be called mere desires, because these desires are completely 'steady', remaining unchanged until your last breath. Honestly, these desires are the very life source of a human being. The point I am emphasising is that everyone has three desires that they must live for and even die for. At the same time, I am trying to drive home the point that desires are the root cause of sorrow no matter what, because there is no guarantee of them being fulfilled, but yes, one is sure to be gripped by sorrow if they remain unfulfilled. That is why nurturing futile desires is dangerous! Spirituality, in fact, has long called

In life, you cannot 'determine' the actions you will or won't perform. It is always 'life' that determines this

'desire' the greatest enemy of a human being, and not without reason. For, it is the countless desires that obstruct life from progressing in one direction and give rise to new confusions every day. But make no mistake—I am not speaking of your futile desires. I'm speaking of the 'three core desires' which are the life source of a human being—his very lifeline. And once your lifeline is severed, everything comes to an end. So, I urge you, live for these three desires, and also be willing to die for them. When everything including your life and death starts revolving around them, you will find the purpose of your life in the form of these desires. And once you start living for a definite purpose, you will never engage in the futile exercise of expanding thoughts and desires, because you will become so engrossed in these core desires that you will have absolutely no time to look elsewhere. And once you do this, the majority of your confusions will vanish in an instant.

Comprehend clearly that the three desires I am discussing are 'inherent' in a human being. They are not adopted or imposed through external influences or compulsions. They arise from within and are as much a part of you as your arms, legs, kidney or liver. However, since only a handful of people are aware of the three-dimensional theory of Nature, very few are able to discern these 'three innate desires'. Truth be told, man's inability to recognise these three deep-seated desires is leading him astray, causing him to deviate from his true path in life. For, these desires are his life and can also rightly be called the purpose of his life.

At present, understand that failing to identify your three core desires is no doubt a serious issue, but even if someone recognises his desires and

Those who refrain from using their intelligence are the very people who become religious or socially acceptable

wants to pursue them, it is still not easy. Imagine a child who dreams of becoming a musician, but is pressured by his parents to become a doctor. Or a child who finds meaning in cricket, but is discouraged by his family. Even otherwise, human beings have an innate tendency to control and dictate the lives of others. Whether it is family, society or religious institutions, everyone has busied themselves with attacking the personal lives of others. Any kind of compulsion or imposition on others is inherently wrong, but who will reason with them? Since they lack psychological awareness, they fail to understand that only a human being himself can identify his three core desires. Additionally, they fail to understand that as soon as man forsakes his three 'core desires', he becomes as good as 'dead'. But despite this, they continue to force their will upon him. However, it is imperative to realise that the three core desires of a human being are not some 'empty or baseless desires', but in fact, his innate personality, and the 'death' of one's personality is no different from one's actual death. Indeed, everyone needs to understand that as soon as an individual's personality dies, he becomes nothing but a 'living corpse'. Sadly, most people today are wandering through life this way—alive, but dead inside. Therefore, I have to emphatically state that you must not force or impose your will upon others.

To state this simply, according to the three-dimensional theory of Nature, three core desires are ingrained in every human being, and every individual has a natural affinity towards them. The only difference is: some recognise these desires, while others remain totally oblivious to them. If you truly want to fathom this matter in depth, look back at your 'childhood' as it will help bring clarity regarding these desires. This is because when it comes to core desires, most people share a similar story—the only difference being, some people are more inclined towards their desires, while some have a weaker proclivity. Generally speaking, most children in their early years, especially between the ages of ten and eighteen, are drawn towards these desires and also express them wholeheartedly. In fact, they even try their best to live by those desires, sometimes by fiercely fighting against external pressures to protect their desires. However, gradually, they begin to let go of these 'desires', sometimes by succumbing to the adversities of life and at other times, by yielding to family pressure. Sometimes, they come under the influence of societal and religious groups too. And out of those who persevere and manage to safeguard their desires until adulthood, many abandon them after marriage. For, the pressure and expectations of a life partner can override even the strongest inner voice. In short, only a few remain loyal to their core desires throughout their lives. As for the vast majority, they unfortunately surrender, be it due to circumstances or some other external pressure. The key point is that the majority of people fail to live in alignment with their 'core desires'.

Now, don't bring up the nonsensical argument that if one has to live in this world, one must listen to everyone and heed their counsel. Do not even complain that the compulsions of life force you into choices you never wanted. The truth is, man is not helpless. If you surrender, it is only because of your own weaknesses. Look through the pages of history—only those who remained steadfast in the pursuit of their desires have left an indelible mark on this world, despite bearing hardships and leading a penurious life, without a roof over their head or a morsel of food in their stomach. Only those who stood firm against the world to follow their passion have gone on to create history. So, please don't ever mistake your weaknesses to be the compulsions of life.

That said, let me explain why I'm focusing so much on the fulfilment of these three core desires. Why are they so important? Well, it's because Nature has its own secret behind sowing the seeds of these desires in human beings. Answer this: since we humans are deeply creative beings, on what basis can we be 'differentiated' from one another? Cows and buffaloes may all live the same way, but humans, gifted with creativity, would obviously not live identical lives. So, where does the variety come from? It is not as if one human being has four limbs and another has twenty! Having different names also does not set us apart from one another. Variety in the creative human species is only possible at the 'mental level'; and verily, the three core desires each of us carries are what differentiate one human being from another. They are the reason Gautam Buddha is vastly different from Walt Disney. So, a person must live for these three desires and also be willing to die for them. For, they are not random desires—they are your life's purpose. In fact, they are a human being's introduction and also his identity in this world. When you lose them, you lose your reason for living. Just as a body cannot live without blood, a human being cannot live with a heart devoid of desires. These innate desires are flowing through you like lifeblood. Hence, you must live for them, and if needed, be ready to die for them. You are human—you are powerful. So, don't surrender. Remain steadfast; struggle if you must. Lose whatever else but never lose your personality i.e. your three core desires. Because once you abandon them, the pain will follow you forever. It will neither allow you to live in peace nor let you die peacefully. And if you are someone who has forsaken these desires, you must surely be experiencing that pain this very moment, for any victim of this pain always experiences a strange kind of restlessness. He forgets what it is like to experience joy! He remains sad and lost and struggles to stay focused, losing interest in everything, and due to all this, his behaviour becomes confusing and erratic. And this is not a good sign at all. Truth be told, this disconnection from one's core desires is one of the biggest reasons people 'lose their way in life' and are 'riddled with confusion'.

The larger problem, however, is that very few people are aware of Nature's 'three-dimensional theory'. Had they been aware, the very first lesson taught to a child would be to identify his three core desires—because those desires are the very 'purpose' of his life.

Secondly, everyone around him would have supported and encouraged him to pursue them. But for this to happen, the world must first fathom the mysteries of Nature. And that will take time! For now, just understand that these desires are deeply rooted in every human being, and generally, we feel a strong urge to pursue them until around the age of eighteen. Even you, in your childhood, must have felt an inclination towards some pursuits. So, what goes wrong after that? Well, people start losing touch with their desires, either because they never fully identified them or because of life's compulsions, external pressures and influences. In other words, their desires stop being their priority and fail to become the purpose of their life. Whatever the case may be, grasp well that these desires don't die or weaken. On the contrary, they haunt a person because they are an inherent part of his personality. This is why I insist that you must identify your three core desires and pursue them lifelong.

And no, I'm not trying to instigate you—actually, that is exactly what I am doing. Because every human being has the right to live the life they truly desire—the one they've dreamt of. Ending your life isn't the only form of suicide; suppressing your heart and mind is also a kind of suicide. The body dies once, but on the mental plane, a person can die numerous deaths every day. So, don't take this lightly. Never allow your desires to be suppressed, and never try to suppress someone else's either. That, in essence, is true 'humanity'. All other notions people preach in the name of humanity are just fanciful stories. The moment desires are crushed, a person begins to wither inside. They become irritable, lost in thought and behave in ways even they don't understand. Why? Because when someone's desires are suppressed, they turn into a living corpse, and such behaviour is typical of corpses. So, ask yourself: if life becomes devoid of 'life-nurturing desires', how will that person ever be able to perform any task 'wholeheartedly'? They won't. They'll drift through life—restless, upset and frustrated. Here, let me point out that we are only talking about the 'three main natural desires', so don't bring in random or superficial wants in this discussion.

To summarise, everyone has the right to nurture their three main desires in life without causing impediments in others' path. It is, in fact, everyone's 'duty' to fulfil their three core desires without becoming a burden on anyone else. And for that purpose, it is important to both recognise those desires and also muster the courage to fulfil them. Nevertheless, it is obvious that most people have given up on their desires, which is why the world feels full of lifeless individuals. But does that mean it's too late? Absolutely not. Nothing is ever truly lost. Even now, you can reconnect with your desires and retrace your steps. Regardless of the reason you have suppressed them, you must find your way back to them if you see a chance. And even for those who have forsaken their desires and have come a long way or have absolutely no inkling of their desires, there is still a solution. They must make note of the 'three desires' as per their present circumstances, the ones that have the potential of being fulfilled, and pursue them from today onwards. This time, don't give in to weaknesses. Maybe you gave up once, but don't make the same mistake again, for you may not get a third chance. Thus, taking into consideration the burning desire within and your external circumstances, carefully choose your 'three new core desires'. The moment you introduce these 'new desires' in your life, you will feel re-energised. You will no longer feel lost, anxious or depressed. Moreover, you will be rid of confusing behaviour as well. Most importantly, your life will embark on a single determined path. Once you start living with

The game of life is simple—in this world, nothing can be gained for free

the intent of fulfilling your three desires, you will be rid of not just confusing behaviour but confusion too. Because now, both you and others will realise that these three desires are your priority. So, you won't feel confused, and others too will not be confused about you. I truly hope you will take this opportunity to make a fresh start and put in the required effort.

Understand clearly that when people disconnect from their three core desires, the fire blazing within them snuffs out. Consequently, they become like dull machines trapped in a monotonous existence. Observe carefully and you will notice a stark contrast between their childhood enthusiasm and their present state. The joy, excitement and spark are all gone. What you see instead is someone who seems lost, uninterested and confused. These aren't signs of a person who is truly alive—these are signs of a living corpse, someone whose existence is reduced to just breathing. Imagine someone whose true passion is dance, but life forces him into a storekeeper's job. What do you think will happen? He won't be able to take his mind off dance, nor give his all to his job. His body may be present in the shop, but his mind will be stuck elsewhere. Eventually, he will feel mentally numb, disconnected and unable to act with clarity. He will remain lost in thought and eventually slip into depression. In other words, his behaviour will become extremely confusing. The same holds true for a foodie who is forced to live on a strict, joyless diet. Simply stated, as soon as a person's three main desires are suppressed, he turns into a living corpse and his behaviour becomes confusing too. And we now know how harmful this is. Therefore, identify your three main desires and live to fulfil them. This will ensure the spark in your life remains alive and you will no longer be confused about your life. Indeed, when you live your life in complete alignment with your desires, how will you ever be gripped by confusion? Even if life throws a thousand options at you, you will invariably 'choose' and prioritise your three main desires. This is what it means to live with purpose. And once you start living for your purpose, all your confusions will be gone. And all that will remain is desires...desires...and desires.

Practical Application

To make sure this message stays with you, go through the practical application given below. If you're still in the early stages of your life and your desires are still alive, list them in the chart below. But if you have suppressed your desires and moved ahead in life, then based on your present circumstances and the fire still burning inside you, define 'three new desires' and list them here. Then, make a firm resolve that you will live for these desires. Don't let anyone or anything stop you from fulfilling them. Whenever you feel your resolve weaken, read this chart which you have filled yourself. Let it remind you of what truly matters and reignite your determination. Then, just watch your life transform in wondrous ways. For, your life has now become focused, and only a person living a focused life can make concentrated efforts—and in today's world, we all know how impactful focused effort can be. Simply put, living with the sole purpose of fulfilling your three core desires unlocks countless benefits. But even after understanding this, if you still choose not to live for them...well, what more can I say?

So, do not miss this once-in-a-lifetime opportunity. Fill in the chart below and start your life afresh. Remember, these three desires are your lifeline. They are your 'Brahma-Vishnu-Mahesh'—your Creator, Sustainer and Destroyer. In other words, they are your whole and soul. Without them, you are just a confused machine—alive but rudderless. Notice carefully, the world is full of such confused beings. But you must not become one of them. And to that effect, never forget that although you can do a great many things, you cannot go against yourself even if you wish to. Essentially, you are the sum total of your 'three main natural desires'. The moment you abandon them, you lose yourself. But when you recognise and embrace them and flow with them, joy and success will naturally find their way into your life, much like Meera's everlasting ecstasy and Krishna's phenomenal progress. So, take this seriously because these desires are your life force. Now, how much more can I encourage or motivate you? So, fill in the chart and fill yourself with determination to start living for your three core desires.

No.	Your three main desires	'Obstacles' you might have to encounter in pursuing those desires	Write determinedly that I will not allow these obstacles to crush my 'desires'
1.	....	....	....
2.	....	....	....
3.	....	....	....

Is It Possible
to Vanquish Confusion Completely?

So far, we have explored and comprehended the significant causes of confusion and confusing behaviour, along with ways to overcome them. If these insights are implemented correctly, one can certainly free oneself from both confusion and confusing behaviour. Nevertheless, the question remains—can confusion be vanquished entirely? Is it truly possible to live a life free of confusion? To answer this, I have already explained earlier that the answers to all the profound mysteries of life are available in Nature. All one needs to do is sharpen one's 'psycho-spiritual insight'. So, here's an exercise for you. Lift your gaze to the sky—look at Nature. Dedicate at least half an hour every morning to observe the sky and continue this quiet practice until you begin to fathom the 'psychological existence' of confusion. Truly speaking, this is all the knowledge one needs to imbibe. Once you learn to make these profound observations, clarity will set in and the everyday matters of life will become crystal clear. Remember, chances like these—to awaken a deeper awareness—are rare, so don't let this opportunity pass you by. Make a sincere attempt to unravel the mystery surrounding confusion on your own.

By now, I trust many of you must have made the necessary effort, and perhaps some have already fathomed the mystery behind confusion. Still, allow me to shed light on this. When you looked at the endless expanse of the sky, you must have noticed the radiant sun, which has been shining uninterrupted for approximately 4.6 billion years, since the moment it came into existence. In other words, it has never paused or stopped engaging in this deed even for a moment. So, tell me, how is it able to do so? Simply because it is not confused about whether it should shine or not. Similarly, look at the Earth. It has been spinning on its axis for over 4.5 billion years without ever faltering. How does it manage such unwavering consistency? Again, it is because it is not confused about its deed.

This illustrates a profound point: a confusion-free existence is indeed possible. You may argue that the sun and planets are celestial bodies—how can we, as human beings, be compared to them? But understand this: the laws that govern the sun and Earth apply equally to us. This means that if the sun and Earth can perform their deeds persistently without yielding to confusion, so can human beings. After all, both entities belong to the same universe. And if you want to delve deeper into how a person can perform deeds consistently without getting trapped in confusion, read the life of Krishna who had performed countless deeds all his life! And truly, what extraordinary feats he had accomplished! Is there anything in this world that he did not achieve? But the question is, how was he able to accomplish so much? It is only because he was not confused about the deeds he had to perform even for a single moment. I can almost hear you protest, "But Krishna was divine, incomparable to us." But why don't you comprehend that whether it is the sun, the Earth or exceptional individuals such as Krishna or Christ, they are all part of this very universe, so how can they be different from you?

Whether it is your spouse's taunts or sulks, bear them with a smile. After all, in exchange for this small cost, you are gaining an invaluable life partner

In essence, life can be lived free of confusion. I have already illustrated this through the examples of the sun, the Earth and the extraordinary life of Krishna. Actually, living a confusion-free life is the very purpose of human existence, for only then can he reach his destination. Once again, I am revealing the ultimate secret of life to you. Just think, what lies at the root of human sorrow and restlessness? Man failing to reach his destination! But have you ever wondered why individuals like Buddha, Vivekananda, Socrates, Picasso and Ghalib are considered great and remembered with reverence? It is because they succeeded in reaching their destination. So, why do so many others flounder aimlessly? Well, the sole reason is confusion. Remember, human life is finite. A person has limited time at his disposal, and only when he performs his deeds in this time span can he assuredly reach his destination. Consider a simple analogy: a Delhi-bound train departs from Mumbai—a journey that takes sixteen hours. Naturally, the train has only sixteen hours to complete its journey. So, when will it arrive at its destination? Only when it runs the entire duration of sixteen hours. Now imagine that the train becomes confused—unsure of its route, hesitant in its movement, veering off course. It will never reach Delhi. This example, though simple, makes the point abundantly clear: to reach one's destination, confusion must be overcome completely. I have shared a deep insight with you, so make the most of it. No one becomes great by merely declaring an intention to be great. A person will attain 'greatness' only when he flows in alignment with the laws of Nature. So, let us now explore ways to triumph over confusion completely.

Determine the Purpose of Life

The very fact that life exists means there must be some purpose to it. And the word 'purpose' implies that it can only be 'one'. Do not wrongly assume multiple objectives or frequently changing goals to be your 'purpose'. The word 'purpose' implies that it is unique to everyone and deeply personal too. Let me also clarify that if you consider something to be the purpose of your life, it naturally assumes the highest priority in your life. Then, it leaves no room for confusion. The key point I want to underline is: every individual must have one such 'topmost priority' in life.

Well, this was one aspect to consider. Another noteworthy point is that if life has a purpose, then it becomes vital to gain clarity about it as early as possible. Ideally, one should identify the purpose of their life in the formative stages of life. And this is not very difficult because 'purpose' implies everyone's 'personal goal' in life, and to achieve this personal goal is the ultimate destination for a human being. And the 'burning desire' to reach his destination is already present in every human being. It is natural. It is inborn. Unfortunately, in the face of external pressures and influences, this fire often dies out. And the moment it dies, a person begins to engage in all kinds of pointless pursuits. An even greater truth is that once someone bows to external influences and pressures, they fall in that trap repeatedly. And with every new influence, they adopt a 'new purpose'. This implies, a matter that was purely personal has now become public, and because it has become public, their life is now flooded with an 'avalanche of purposes'. With time, their 'main purpose' fades away, lost beneath a pile of other purposes, and interestingly, they don't even realise this. Exhausted and disoriented, they begin to drift, leading a purposeless life...and a life devoid of purpose is always riddled with confusion. Sadly, this is the condition most people find themselves in today, and this is especially tragic given the advanced age we live in.

Broadly speaking, a person who discovers the purpose of his life i.e. his 'personal goal', is the only one who can triumph over confusion. Look around: the sun, the Earth, the wind, the water—every element of Nature operates with a single purpose. That is why none of them experience confusion; in other words, they have triumphed over confusion. And you are no different from them, for you too are a part of this universe. You too can 'live with a single purpose', and in doing so, conquer confusion once and for all. So, this reaffirms that a confusion-free life is indeed possible.

Allow me to explain further by sharing the examples of a few remarkable individuals, the ones who have left an indelible mark on the world. Perhaps, through their stories, you may be able to relate better. Take Walt Disney, for instance. Since childhood, he recognised that his true calling lay in drawing and animation. Once he identified this as his life's purpose, it naturally became his topmost priority, leaving no scope for any other option. This meant there was no room for confusion. So, without getting confused, he devoted himself to every deed that brought him 'closer to his purpose' while consciously avoiding those that took him 'further away from his purpose'. In a similar manner, Thomas Edison dedicated his life to scientific discovery, his every waking moment revolving around experimentation and invention. When Buddha renounced a life of luxury, he did so to pursue a single purpose: the search for truth. And when the purpose is determined, the choice is clear too. Then, there is no need to waver, no reason to look elsewhere. I'm sure you must have now grasped that the one who lives with a single purpose triumphs over confusion. And this isn't limited to just the sun and the Earth; countless great people have indeed led their lives with 'a single purpose'.

Let us now consider the example of Krishna, whose sole purpose in life was to work for the 'greater good'. And once the purpose was chosen, there was no place for confusion. In an age lacking modern scientific tools and technologies, the means to benefit mankind took a different form. In those times, if one's

Life is a business, so treat it as one. Never miss out on paying a lesser price to gain something of greater value

purpose of life was to work for the greater good, one could do it only by annihilating sinners. For, once the tyrants were eliminated, peace and harmony could prevail among the common people. Thus, Krishna made the annihilation of sinners his purpose in life. Then, he never found himself confused about the moral implications of how he could slay his own uncle, Kansa. He thus courageously vanquished his cruel uncle without an iota of confusion. Krishna loved Radha deeply, but never allowed that love to override his purpose of purging the world of sinners. Although he enjoyed the luxuries and grandeur of Dwarka, his sole priority was to decimate sinners. His passions in life—music, dance, food and the flute—were dear to him, but he did not become so engrossed in them that he would deviate from the main purpose of his life. Whether it was Radha or Dwarka, Krishna willingly walked away from both whenever they stood in the way of his purpose. In short, whenever the annihilation of sinners became the need of the hour, he sacrificed everything he held dear, without ever losing the serene smile on his face. And so, I ask you: how can a person with such unwavering determination towards his purpose ever be confused about his *karma* (actions)?

Now, understand why confusion takes hold of you in the first place. In today's world, you are surrounded by endless choices—countless directions in which to go and endless things to pursue. And naturally, when one sees unlimited options, one becomes confused. And as long as this ocean of options exists, confusion will exist too. But for someone who has already chosen his life's purpose, how can there be any option? Whenever he is confronted with a choice, he will invariably choose his purpose. This implies—

Even on his deathbed, a human being has to engage in profitable interactions —otherwise, he cannot even die a 'peaceful death'

no option, no confusion. I hope you have now understood why those who live with a single purpose are not confused.

In other words, for someone who lives with a single purpose, their purpose is everything, much like a compass that guides every action, every decision. However, that doesn't mean they don't do anything else in life. They certainly don't abandon their hobbies, pleasure or the richness of life. Life must undoubtedly be lived to the fullest, but their purpose remains the priority. When faced with a choice, they always choose their purpose without hesitation. Yes, such people may still face light-hearted, everyday confusions—like whether to have pani puri or samosa, whether to listen to music or watch a movie. But these are harmless confusions, the playful indecisions that add flavour and variety to life. In fact, those who don't have such pleasant confusions in their life lead a dull, monotonous and restricted life. "This is all we will eat, all we will drink and all we will do!" is their oft-repeated refrain. However, you must never lead such a dull life! Don't fear small confusions, for they are actually quite pleasurable, filling life with happiness. What you must avoid is confusion about the major decisions of life, the ones that impact your entire life.

The crux of the matter is, if you want to triumph over confusion, seek a purpose in life—the primary 'reason' for your existence. That 'reason' will automatically eliminate the rest of your confusions. Let me also clarify here that age or circumstances can never stop you from wanting to live with a single purpose. The only real barriers are a lack of vision or determination. Otherwise, rest assured, you can find the purpose of your life at any stage.

In short, 'living with a single purpose' is the most straightforward solution to triumph over confusion. Just as the sun shines, the wind blows, and water flows with one specific purpose, humans too have their 'own individual purpose'. Only those who haven't identified their purpose or have surrendered it due to some reason will find themselves mired in confusion. This is a profound truth I have stated, so grasp it well. Once you embrace it in its entirety, it will surely ignite within you 'the fire to seek the purpose of life'. For now, simply know this: you have come into this world for a specific purpose. So, ignite within yourself the fervour—the fire—to find that purpose. And if you have strayed too far from it, find a new purpose. But whatever you do, start living with a single purpose as soon as possible. The day you do, you will begin to enjoy life like never before. And as an added bonus, you will also be rid of confusion.

At first glance, living with a single purpose might seem simple—even appealing in its clarity. But practically speaking, it is quite challenging. And remaining steadfast in the pursuit of your purpose is no cakewalk either. Unless you conquer the frailties of your mind, this will not be possible. This is precisely why a complete victory over confusion is not easy. To live with a single purpose means that your purpose becomes your supreme priority. When life forces you to choose between health and purpose, you must choose your purpose. You must give importance to your health only to the extent that it is essential to 'achieve your purpose'. Similarly, if the choice is between loss of wealth and purpose, you must willingly endure the loss of wealth. Even when the choice is between God and your purpose, you must still choose your purpose. If your purpose constantly takes a backseat to fame, reputation, wealth or is being influenced by religion or health, then do not mistake this for living with a single purpose. Look at the lives of those who achieved greatness. Reflect on the immense trials that Buddha endured on his path to achieve his purpose. Consider how many of his near and dear ones Krishna abandoned for his purpose. Think about the losses and setbacks faced by visionaries like Thomas Edison and Walt Disney in achieving their purpose. The very essence of purpose is that anyone who comes in its way will inevitably face defeat. And this is only possible when the 'fire of purpose' roars inside you. Without that fire, your purpose will be defeated daily by everything and everyone. Furthermore, it will change as quickly as your moods.

You've probably met people who declare a new purpose every time you see them, but I sincerely hope you will not become one of them.

Undeniably, it is not easy to devote your entire life to a single purpose. It requires a fierce inner fire, fuelled by the courage to remain undeterred. Hence, it must be acknowledged that living for a single purpose is definitely not a feat that everyone can achieve. This journey might take some time, and to even evoke this emotion within oneself is remarkable in itself. To nurture and fuel that fire, you will need to become psychologically powerful, because every day will bring with it a new test. Indeed, if you wish to stick to one purpose with determination, you will have to deal with the 'challenges of the external world and the trials of life' on a daily basis. And to do that, you will have to not only read profound psychology, but also absorb and internalise it. Only then the fire of living for that one single purpose will be ignited within you. That said, it doesn't mean that if you haven't yet found or committed to a single purpose, your life is meaningless. Not at all! But understand this: to live with no purpose is to live in perpetual confusion. You will aimlessly meander through life, switching directions every so often, and ultimately finding yourself at the same point from where you had begun. You will start a hundred things but succeed in none; build countless relationships but struggle to sustain even one; weave countless dreams but fail to fulfil even one. Therefore, we must not live in a state of confusion, come what may. And the only way to alleviate your confusions is to start living with a single purpose. There is no other foolproof solution to triumph over confusion.

If the idea of living for a single purpose with unwavering determination feels overwhelming to

What money can buy and what conduct earns are entirely different. And both are essential to live a complete life

you, I would suggest an easier approach. It is perfectly okay if you are not yet ready to dedicate yourself to one clear purpose. The real challenge in life is confusion, as it is due to confusion that you are unable to perform any deed determinedly, causing much of your time to be wasted in inaction. And without taking decisive action, how will your life progress? How will you reach your destination if you're constantly changing direction? That is why freeing yourself from confusion is not just important—it is urgent. Being in a state of confusion is a clear-cut proof that your life is not heading in the right direction. Conversely, a confusion-free life is a guarantee that you are marching successfully towards your destination. So, you must ensure you triumph over confusion at any cost. To help you do that, let me offer a simpler, more approachable method. Start by turning inwards. Spend a few days in solitude if you must, but use that time for deep introspection. Look within and seek your innermost, core desires. Keep in mind that I'm not speaking of the inflated desires of ego or ambition, but of your genuine innermost desires. Once you have introspected deeply, write down four desires. Choose two that bring you joy and happiness such as your hobbies, passions or leisure pursuits. Then choose two more that are related to your work i.e. desires that have the potential to shape your future. In short, choose what brings you joy and what gives your work meaning. Then, simply begin to live your life centred around these two kinds of deeds. Make them your topmost priority. And when other tempting options appear, choose these desires only, over and over. Let me be clear: I'm not asking you to choose a target. A target is an external outcome, like earning a certain amount of money or gaining a certain status. That is ambition, whereas I am

A confusion-free life achieves such phenomenal feats that one day, the entire world salutes it

suggesting that you choose your desires. For example, if your desire is to sing, then singing becomes your topmost priority. In such a case, there is no target of attaining fame or wealth through your renditions. If you harbour any such notions, you would once again deviate from your path. And verily, the vast majority has already deviated! Besides, if your wish is to earn money or achieve name and fame, it no longer remains your desire; in that case, your desire has turned into a target. Psychologically speaking, 'desire' is internal while 'target' is external. The two are completely distinct from each other. And if your target is to achieve fame or wealth, how will the 'fire for your desires' remain alive within you? In such a scenario, whenever you find financial gain in some other work, you will immediately change your line of work for monetary gain. Therefore, I am certainly not discussing those who set targets; I am referring to desires, not targets. Hence, do not confuse me and avoid being confused yourself. Remember, Picasso had chosen his 'desire' for painting. Ghalib had chosen poetry. Edison had chosen science experiments, while Disney had chosen drawing and animation. In other words, each one of them had chosen their desire for their work pursuits, not targets. And that's what I'm asking of you: make the choice of pursuing your desire and not your targets. Confusion belongs to those who choose targets, for they simply cannot follow a single path. Truth be told, they spend their lives making bold declarations but accomplishing little. However, we are not discussing such people at the moment.

Now, coming back to our central point, once you have chosen two desires linked to your work and two rooted in your personal interests or hobbies, let them become your 'topmost priority' as you forge ahead in their pursuit without deviating from your path. Steer clear of anything that obstructs these desires, and wholeheartedly welcome everything that strengthens and supports them. With this effort on your part, you will free yourself from confusion permanently. And here's the beautiful part: you have chosen desires that not only enhance your career and future but also bring joy and personal fulfilment, which means you have naturally begun to live a purposeful, well-rounded life—one that balances work and pleasure in a harmonious rhythm. Well, what more could you ask for?

Once you have begun this journey, pursuing these four desires with unwavering determination, the next step is to reflect deeply on your relationships. Choose, in your heart, four individuals who matter the most to you, and make it a priority to cherish them and their happiness and well-being. In essence, let your life purpose include two meaningful work pursuits, two joyful hobbies and four cherished relationships. With this approach, confusion will begin to dissipate and life will start to flow seamlessly. For those who find it overwhelming to live for a single purpose, this method offers a practical alternative. That said, let me remind you: living with a single purpose is the most powerful, transformative way to live. What we have discussed here is just an alternative method to eliminate confusion.

One important aspect to keep in mind when adopting the second method is that occasionally, you might have to face some obstacles, simply because you no longer have one single purpose but eight. Naturally, this may sometimes lead to a clash between your hobbies and your relationships, or between your hobbies and work pursuits. Although, this would be rare. But in such moments, do not let indecision overwhelm you. Simply choose what feels most important in that moment. Trust that what you've chosen was the right decision for that situation, and what you've set aside was necessary to let go of. This small but conscious shift in mindset will also help you navigate confusion to a large extent. That said, life is unpredictable. There may be times when an urgent or unexpected matter demands your full attention—something entirely outside your chosen eight pursuits. When that happens, don't resist it. Prioritise the urgent task. Once it is handled, you can return to your eight pursuits. Surely, making such decisions shouldn't be difficult at all.

Nonetheless, to further simplify the process of choosing these eight pursuits, I am providing you with a practical application. This will help you ascertain your purpose properly. But yes, do this only after you have introspected deeply. And remember, your primary focus must be to lead your life with 'a single purpose' so first strive towards that. After all, you were sent into this world to fulfil that one purpose only.

Practical Application – A

No.	Describe your chosen deeds	Write: I resolve that from today onwards, these tasks will remain my top priority
1.	....	....
2.	....	....

Practical Application – B

No.	Describe your chosen hobbies	Write: I will no longer leave a single opportunity to pursue these hobbies
1.	....	....
2.	....	....

Practical Application – C

No.	Describe your chosen relationships	Write: These relationships will remain my top priority
1.	....	....
2.	....	....
3.	....	....
4.	....	....

Using the charts above, you have likely identified two work pursuits, two hobbies and four relationships that matter the most to you. These eight elements now represent your highest priority in life. Yet, some of you might still wonder—why go through the effort of choosing these priorities at all? The answer is simple: to overcome confusion. Confusion stalls action, and without action, how can life flourish? So, it is necessary to select these eight priorities because once you do so, you will stop vacillating and veering off your path. And once your priorities are set, you will no longer 'pause' your deeds in confusion. And that in itself is a powerful foundation for building a remarkable life. Because ultimately, our goal is to shape a truly magnificent life for ourselves.

Yes
a 'Confusion- Free' Life is Possible!

We have clearly understood by now that confusion acts like a speed breaker on the smooth journey of life. It stalls deeds, derails progress and ruins countless lives. When confusion takes hold, neither your talent nor your intelligence helps you—because confusion impairs your ability to perform 'deeds' effectively. Considering the gravity of the situation, we have already discussed several solutions to address it, but now, let us turn towards a solution that approaches confusion differently, eliminating it completely. However, before we do that, let me remind you once again that confusion arises only when there are options. That said, there are people who get confused even when 'there are no options'. However, we are not discussing them. We are focusing on the more common scenario: people who feel confused because they are faced with innumerable choices.

At this point, you might argue, 'But it is quite normal for life to present us with countless options.' And yes, you are absolutely right. When even choosing a career offers so many options, how can one lead a life devoid of options? And, of course, having options is important as it enables one to make the 'best possible choice'. So yes, options are necessary, but the deeper question is: when should you have options, and for what kind of decisions? It is vital to distinguish between the two types of decisions we all face in life. The first type consists of everyday, low-impact decisions—choices that don't leave a lasting impact on your life and neither do they influence your life greatly. For example: Which shirt should you buy? Where should you buy it from? Which restaurant should you visit? Where should you go for a weekend outing? Thousands of such choices have to be made during the course of a day, and in these decisions, one invariably needs options. In fact, the more the options, the better it is! A little confusion here isn't harmful—it's even enjoyable. These are what we might call "pleasant confusions" and they are proof of mankind's progress. But this book isn't concerned with those, nor are we exploring the confusion that arises on account of them. Our focus is on the second kind—the truly significant choices that shape the course of your life. These are the fifty to hundred pivotal decisions of life—the way Arjuna was confused during the Mahabharata war about whether to fight the war or not. In fact, it is similar to a situation wherein someone is pointing a gun at you and you become confused about whether you should save yourself or not. Indeed, what option did Arjuna have in that situation? And honestly speaking, even you do not have many options when making the majority of life's crucial decisions. It is often we who create options where none truly exist.

Returning to the central point of our discussion: wherever there are too many options, confusion is bound to arise. And let's be honest, the world is teeming with choices. So, does that mean living a confusion-free life is impossible? Not at all. Who says you can't live without confusion? You absolutely can. In the absence of options, one can certainly lead a confusion-free existence. Moreover, it is not that you will always have options. Take spontaneity, for example. Are there any options in spontaneity? There aren't any and because there are no options, there is no room for confusion either. It's as clear and simple as the mathematical equation of 2 + 2 = 4.

Now, many of you may very well question, what exactly is spontaneity? Let me assure you—you are not entirely ignorant of it.

You have surely experienced living with spontaneity. In fact, Nature has designed you to live spontaneously. Have you ever paused to consider whether or not you should breathe? Of course not. The thought never arises because there is no option not to breathe. So, in areas where Nature has not provided you with any option, you live spontaneously. You breathe spontaneously, which means you have certainly experienced spontaneity. And this is the point I wish to emphasise—you are not completely unaware of it. Therefore, do not be startled upon hearing the word 'spontaneity'. Moreover, your spontaneity isn't limited to just the act of inhaling and exhaling. On numerous instances, you have displayed even your anger spontaneously. Have you noticed how anger erupts without thought? That's spontaneity too. In such moments, you do not weigh your options—you do not stop to think, 'Should I express this? Should I hold back?' No, you simply act. Why? Because in the heat of that emotion, your mind perceives no other option. And where there is no perception of choice, there is no confusion. This proves that 'options' are indeed the root cause of confusion. The moment multiple options appear, your mind starts analysing, calculating gains and losses and that is when confusion takes hold. However, anger often does not allow room for such considerations, for anger is so powerful that it halts all contemplations. Anger nullifies all calculations of gain and loss. To summarise, when you feel intense anger, it is invariably expressed in a spontaneous manner. In that moment, you simply do not perceive any option apart from expressing your anger.

Did you notice how our conversation which had started with a concept as simple as 'breathing' moved all the way to something as complex as 'anger'! And through this discussion, we have established that not only does one breathe spontaneously, but one often displays anger spontaneously too. It is only due to a lack of deeper psychological understanding that many people are unaware of their inherent spontaneity. But now it has been proven that you are aware of spontaneity and that you also perform 'spontaneous deeds'. And if you start performing all your deeds spontaneously, you would neither look for options nor be mired in confusion. In short, living a confusion-free life is entirely possible if you learn to live spontaneously.

So, that settles the question—is it really possible to live a confusion-free life? But now, a valid concern arises: while a life free from confusion sounds ideal, wouldn't living with total spontaneity border on chaos? Agreed that anger is well beyond our control, but how can everything be done spontaneously? How can one act without thought? How can we go about life without considering consequences, without weighing gain or loss, without thinking about what to embrace and what to let go? Such an approach to life will ruin us completely. In fact, one might argue that it's better to live with confusion than with unchecked spontaneity. Confusion may slow us down, but at least it doesn't throw us off a cliff. And you're absolutely right to think this way. But let's take a step back. I haven't asked you to live spontaneously—at least not yet. The point we were discussing was simply whether a confusion-free life is possible. And in that context, I shared that confusion only arises when options exist. And since spontaneity, by its very nature, has no options, it is indeed possible to live a confusion-free life by living spontaneously. So, there is no need to feel anxious about it.

Now, setting that concern aside, one cannot deny that one has to carve a magnificent life. After all, we are here to figure out how to live such a life. And for that, one thing is absolutely certain—one cannot create a magnificent life without performing deeds, and to do that, you will need to make choices. It is also certain that even when faced with countless options, you can only choose one. And the quicker you make that choice, the better would be your chances of performing more and more deeds. It is also important that your choice is the right one because a wrong choice can set you back significantly. I trust, by now, all these points are clear to you.

Now, we are left with the crucial question: how can we make prompt and accurate decisions about 'what we must do'? So, let me tell you that you are not confused in this matter because nearly all your decisions are made after considerable thought. The premise of decision-making for the majority of people is either their brain or ego. The brain calculates gain and loss—what you stand to win, what you might lose. The ego, on the other hand, is fixated on what others might think, how your choices will be perceived. If you observe closely, you will notice that nearly all your decisions stem from either of these factors. What's more, you approve of this system and you trust it completely. In fact, this is the predominant process taught around the world for 'selection of deeds'.

But this raises an important question: is this process correct? Since the vast majority has been following this process for ages, naturally, very few stop to question it. But here, we will not only question it but also conduct its complete psychoanalysis. Let's begin with the basics. It is clear that your decision-making process is based on either 'gain-loss calculations' or 'what will the world say?' Moreover, the brain doesn't deliver instant answers. It drags you into a maze of endless calculations—what ifs, pros and cons, possible outcomes, all requiring a great amount of time to arrive at a decision. Similarly, the ego, burdened with societal pressure and fear of judgement, also takes its time worrying about opinions, consequences and reputation. This means the process of arriving at a decision in terms of 'selecting deeds' is a time-consuming one, because firstly, it is not easy for the brain to calculate gain-loss as it engages in endless deliberation. Consequently, the majority of time is spent in grappling with the confusion of 'which option should be selected'. And amusingly, after the brain finally makes a selection, the ego rears its head to

Nature has sent humans solely to enjoy this world's bounty—and to make them desire this bounty, it has given them a 'mind'

draw your attention towards 'the opinions of the world'. This means, even after the deed is selected, it is put 'on hold' merely to deliberate over the judgements and opinions of others. Truth be told, during this process of deliberation, the time to perform the deed often slips away. Because by the time you are ready to act, the circumstances have likely changed. Due to this, the majority of your decisions based on calculations of 'gain-loss' and 'external influences and pressures' usually prove to be wrong. So, all said and done, this approach has two drawbacks—first, it wastes precious time in indecisiveness, and second, despite an exhaustive contemplation, decisions ultimately go wrong.

By now, it is evident that most people arrive at their decisions on the strength of the brain-ego. And as we have seen, they waste huge amounts of time calculating potential gains and losses or worrying about what others might think. In other words, their deeds are repeatedly put on 'pause' for extensive periods of time. And ironically, despite all this mental effort, most of their decisions still turn out to be wrong. So, let me ask this: why has no one ever questioned this process? Why hasn't anyone paused to ask, "Is there a better way?" This alone says a lot about how serious everyone is about the precious human life they have been given. If constant calculation of gain-loss and conforming to societal pressures have repeatedly failed us, we should have searched for an alternative method of 'deed-selection'. But despite the pitfalls, no one has stopped to explore other possibilities. This is surprising indeed!

So, let me ask again: why has no one considered other ways of selecting deeds? Why has everyone's focus been limited only to the process of 'contemplation and deliberation' and making calculations of 'gains and losses'? Must every choice be filtered through thinking and analysis? Is it really impossible to decide without deliberation? Despite overwhelming evidence of its ineffectiveness, nearly ninety percent of people still rely on deliberation as their main strategy for navigating life. This is perhaps because they don't even know that an alternative exists. But now we do. We breathe without thinking; we express anger without planning. These are spontaneous actions. So yes, there is an alternative way to make decisions. And let me tell you, this spontaneous way of operating isn't limited to just breathing or expressing anger. Just look at Nature. Do you see the wind pausing to decide where to carry oxygen? Of course not. Yet oxygen reaches every corner of the planet. Have you ever heard that the atmosphere in London failed to produce oxygen resulting in the death of thousands of people? No. In short, deeds are happening without contemplation, and that too, with absolute perfection. The Earth has been spinning on its axis for billions of years without error. What I mean to say is, a single glance at Nature makes us realise that great deeds can certainly be performed spontaneously without undue thinking, contemplation or deliberation.

Well, it is easy to understand that certain human functions like breathing or bursts of anger happen spontaneously. It is also comprehensible that all of Nature's deeds are being accomplished effortlessly without an iota of contemplation. But the crucial question remains: can human beings too perform deeds without conscious deliberation, just like the sun, wind or earth? Leaving aside this question for the time being, it is amply clear that all our internal struggles, from indecision to confusion, arise from unnecessary contemplation. So, whether or not human beings can live spontaneously is a separate matter, but the disadvantages of contemplation and deliberation are quite evident. In fact, there is no room left for debate on this point.

So, what is the alternative? The answer is obvious—spontaneity. And yet, turning to spontaneity feels like walking an uncertain path, as there are no guarantees. How do we know that spontaneity will benefit us? While spontaneity may promise freedom from confusion, can it promise favourable results? Seen from this perspective, living in confusion sounds far better than living spontaneously. Indeed, a pause on deeds is acceptable, but we cannot afford to steer ourselves towards ruin.

The point is pertinent—while spontaneity works effortlessly in the realm of Nature, for human beings, there is no guarantee that embracing spontaneity will always yield favourable outcomes. That is precisely why I haven't yet suggested that you must live spontaneously. All we have established so far is that it is possible to live spontaneously without contemplating minutely over every single matter. Now, let me ask you: why are we having this in-depth discussion? Clearly, to enhance the quality of our lives. And to do that, one thing is obvious: we must make well-informed decisions and that too promptly. I believe there is little disagreement on that point. And there are only two approaches to decision-making: one, careful deliberation and two, spontaneity. No third method exists. And now, we have reached a point in our discussion where we must ask: which of these is more beneficial to us? Because ultimately, we will have to choose the path that best serves us.

I understand that you place immense trust in careful thought and consideration and are hesitant to perform actions without due deliberation. But tell me, what is it that you contemplate? Surely, options. And what do you think about while contemplating? You're assessing which option will serve you best. And on what basis do you carry out that assessment? Through calculating gains and losses and by factoring in how others may perceive your actions. And what is the one thing you need most to do this? Obviously, time. Why? So that you can put the deed on hold while you think it

Even if you have the potential to excel in several fields, you cannot pursue & master them all—simply because you have a limited 'basket of time'

over. This means, you put your actions on hold in every single matter at the slightest instance. If you reflect honestly, you will find something startling: your entire life has been spent in just one deed—putting your actions on hold. Look more closely and you will be shocked to realise—all that you want to accomplish is still 'pending'. So, ask yourself, how will this approach work and how will your life be carved into a great success story if you continue to tread down this path? Therefore, please do not consider 'contemplation and deliberation' to be an exceptional 'quality'. I'm not saying that thinking and contemplation are entirely worthless, but recognise that they amount to nothing more than data analysis. And analysis of data, no matter what kind it is, always demands time. Similarly, in the management and implementation phase of the deed, contemplation and deliberation become essential. However, to contemplate every time before making decisions does not guarantee a formula for success, for how could constantly putting your actions on hold ever be beneficial?

I am well aware that you won't immediately agree with me. So, let's take a closer look at the 'pros and cons' of the process of deliberation. We have already seen that contemplation pauses action, which means deeds are put on hold. Now, tell me, if you pause every single action in order to deliberate, how many actions will be put in limbo? Have you ever calculated this? And how many deeds will remain pending wherein you will never be able to arrive at a decision? I am emphasising this point because most people live like this—relying entirely on contemplation. They even consider it to be an outstanding quality! And so, they put every task on hold to "think it over". But such "intelligent thinkers" never stop to consider how many tasks they have suspended indefinitely. And as you yourself are habituated to constant deliberation, take a moment to think on these points as well. I agree that the habit of thinking and deliberating is deep-rooted in you, which is why it won't be easy to acknowledge its downsides. And this is precisely why I am trying to explain how dangerous the habit of contemplation is.

Alright! Let us set this aside for a moment. If you truly believe in contemplation, then answer this: why do people engage in it? Of course, for their own benefit. No one contemplates with the intention of harming themselves. But surprisingly, no one ever reflects on whether this contemplation is actually serving their interests. Very few evaluate its actual outcome, and that alone indicates the level of their thinking. Clearly, we have never given any thought to the usefulness of contemplation and deliberation, the one thing we rely on the most all our lives. Most people haven't even realised that due to this very habit, they have put nine out of ten deeds on hold. Nor have they taken stock of all the things left undone, forgotten or indefinitely postponed. Neither have they assessed whether the few decisions they did take after due deliberation actually benefited them or not. In short, they haven't reflected on anything that truly matters, yet they find contemplation to be crucial. What's worse, due to the widespread ignorance of psychology in this world, everyone believes that the more they think, the more intelligent they are! Ironically, those who nurse such beliefs have also never delved into the psychoanalysis of 'What are thoughts?', 'Where do they come from?' or 'Why do we overthink?' Indeed, they are so 'intelligent' that they have never given a thought to the number of confusions that arise due to excessive thinking and deliberation, but continue to confidently declare: 'Whatever you do, do it after careful deliberation.'

Through our discussion so far, we have at least succeeded in casting serious doubt on the so-called importance of contemplation and deliberation. After the detailed explanation above, it should be clear to you that contemplation offers 'no guarantee of making the right decision'. Thinking deeply before taking any action may seem wise, but it certainly doesn't mean it's a foolproof method. Given the pitiable state of most people's lives, it doesn't seem that this approach has any advantages. But regardless of that, life must be carved into something grand and meaningful. And for that, one has no option but to perform deeds. Now, if we were to ignore the process of contemplation-deliberation, then we are left with only one alternative method of deed selection: spontaneity. And the reason I had raised so many questions around contemplation-deliberation was to prepare you to genuinely engage with the idea of spontaneity. If contemplation can no longer be trusted as a fool-proof method, then we owe it to ourselves to explore spontaneity in its complete depth, and I'm sure you will now show a keen interest in understanding spontaneity. So, similar to 'contemplation-deliberation', let us delve into a complete psychoanalysis of spontaneity as well. After all, if one approach has shown its limitations, what is the harm in considering the other? Who knows, perhaps spontaneity holds the very key we've been seeking.

So, what exactly are spontaneous deeds? Spontaneous deeds basically mean that you performed an action based on the tempest that raged within you, without forethought, and the results became evident to you after the deed was done. In other words, there is no deliberation or careful thought involved in such a deed. There is no calculation or assessment of whether the deed is favourable or unfavourable. Furthermore, there are no 'external pressures, impositions or influences' that dictate whether you should or should not perform this deed. In short, there is no 'confusion' about whether you should perform the deed or not simply because the deed occurs first and you become aware of 'what you did' later. These are what we call 'spontaneous deeds'.

At first glance, such deeds can seem risky, maybe even reckless. I'm sure many of you must have felt a sense of discomfort or even a shiver down your spine after reading the description of spontaneous deeds—while many of you have already shown suspicion or doubt about spontaneity. But this is only because we have never conducted its in-depth psychoanalysis. Indeed, when even the science of thought and contemplation is so difficult to grasp, how will anyone be able to fathom spontaneity easily? However, when there are only two ways of performing actions, it becomes essential to fully understand both, especially considering the fact that 'actions' or 'deeds' are the very foundation of one’s life.

Well, we have conducted a thorough psychoanalysis of ‘contemplation’ and have gained a fair understanding of what constitutes a spontaneous deed as well. It is now evident that regardless of the nature of the deed being performed, it will be driven either by contemplation or spontaneity. There is no third method of performing deeds. And to clarify, there is no ‘hybrid’ model that merges the two; each deed belongs clearly to one category or the other. With this understanding, I would like to make a simple request: first, reflect on whether you engage in any spontaneous deeds at all. If you do, try to assess how often you perform deeds spontaneously in comparison to deeds guided by thoughtful deliberation. Indeed, before moving forward, it is essential to check where you currently stand, and to help you do that, I have given you a practical application. In the chart below, list ten major decisions that you have made, and next to those, write whether you took the decision spontaneously or after due deliberation. Although this exercise won’t provide a complete picture, it will certainly offer a valuable insight into your decision-making tendencies—specifically, the percentage of decisions you made after due deliberation and the percentage of decisions you made spontaneously in the key areas of your life.

Practical Application

No.	Write about the important decisions you have taken	Note down whether those decisions were made through contemplation or spontaneity
1.	....	....

2.	....	....
3.	....	....
4.	....	....
5.	....	....
6.	....	....
7.	....	....
8.	....	....
9.	....	....
10.	....	....

Now that you have filled this chart, you must have realised that most of your significant decisions were made through contemplation and deliberation. In all likelihood, you did not choose your academic stream spontaneously—you probably considered your options carefully, sought guidance and did your research to ensure you are making the right decision. Similarly, your marriage must have also been a decision taken after due deliberation. Indeed, it is a long-standing teaching that one must not perform any action without due deliberation. But now, take a step back and ask yourself honestly: has your life flourished the way it should have? Is it progressing the way you had hoped? Have you achieved what you believe you were truly capable of, given your potential and talents? Check whether you are receiving less than what your talent merits in every sphere of your life. Ask yourself: don't you deserve a far better existence than the one you are presently leading? Most probably, you do! And it is, indeed, unfortunate that the majority of people have received far less than they deserve from the reservoir of life. This brings us to a crucial question: why is this so? At the very least, make an effort to seek the answer to this question, because truly, what could be more important than understanding why you are receiving less than your potential.

So, setting everything else aside, give this question the priority it warrants. Reflect deeply: Why haven't things unfolded in line with your talent and efforts? Who or what is responsible for this? Is it God, destiny, vaastu shaastra (ancient science that unifies art, astronomy and astrology), *karma* (deeds), past *karma* (past deeds), family, friends, circumstances or something else entirely? Clearly, something isn't adding up. For, despite having the potential, things are not working out for you. And since this question concerns your life, the answer will have to be found, come what may. So, introspect deeply and, in the chart below, note down the five key reasons you believe are responsible for you receiving less than what you are truly capable of in life. Instead of living in unawareness, it is better to conduct an in-depth analysis of your life thus far. So, I urge you to approach this exercise sincerely and thoughtfully.

No.	**Describe in detail the five main reasons you believe are responsible for you receiving less than what your talent and potential warrant**
1.	....

2.	....
3.	....
4.	....
5.	....

Undoubtedly, with the help of the charts above, you must have thoroughly analysed your life, an exercise that will prove immensely valuable in the long run. While the full impact of this reflection will unfold gradually, we have now gained a clear understanding of how decisions are made, whether spontaneously or through contemplation and careful deliberation. Here's the crux of what we've learnt: spontaneous decisions seem risky, but even the decisions made after thorough deliberation are failing to deliver great results. So, what are we to do? Should we stop making decisions altogether? That is not a viable option. For, choosing inaction will only risk losing whatever progress we have made so far. So, what is the way forward? You might be tempted to say, "Wait a minute, isn't this book supposed to help eliminate confusion? Yet, here I am, more confused than before!" But don't worry—we are still very much on track, discussing ways to secure a complete victory over confusion. It just requires a bit of patience. After all, confusion is no trivial matter.

So far, we have established that a deed can be performed either spontaneously or after due deliberation. The next step is to understand the fundamental difference between these two approaches. For that, I want you to carefully read the chart below, after which you will not be confused about either of these methods.

Deeds performed spontaneously	Deeds performed after due deliberation
They happen naturally without any consideration of gain or loss.	These deeds are based solely on calculations of gain and loss.
There is no room for contemplation or pause in these deeds.	Deeds are put on hold in order to contemplate and deliberate.
There is absolutely no room for confusion in these deeds.	There is always a sense of confusion in these deeds.
These deeds have no scope for calculations of benefit-loss or deliberation-contemplation.	Contemplation is done precisely to avoid losses and secure benefits.
These deeds are completely devoid of calculations.	These deeds involve extensive calculations.
These deeds are free from external pressures and influences.	These deeds are majorly impacted by external pressures and influences.
A human being has no control over such deeds.	A human being has complete control over these deeds.

By now, you have gained a clear understanding of the difference between spontaneous deeds and those performed after contemplation and deliberation. You must have also recognised that the majority of your deeds fall into the second category. This naturally raises the question: why do most people rely solely on deliberation to perform their deeds? What is the primary reason behind this? There must be something compelling that convinces them that this is the right way to make decisions or that there is no better approach than this. Surely, there must be some starting point from which all contemplation arises. So, what is it? What makes contemplation essential? I will explain this point, but before I do, I invite you to pause and reflect on it yourself. Believe me, these seemingly small instances of introspection will significantly strengthen your psychological power. And make no mistake: if there is one thing you truly need to build an extraordinary life, it is 'psychological power'. So, before reading further, take a moment to consider: Why does contemplation feel so essential? What is that one thing that drives you—and everyone else—to engage in excessive thinking and contemplation?

Well, let me tell you, the 'concern for one's own benefit' is the starting point of all contemplations. Without this concern, no one would feel the need to weigh options or deliberate before making a choice. And really, is there anyone who isn't concerned about their own benefit? And why shouldn't one be? If you don't look after your own interests, who else will? It's a fair point—one that I fully agree with. I also agree that in order to safeguard one's interests, contemplation is necessary. Without thinking things through, it seems impossible to protect one's interests.

So, it is clear that everyone's top priority in life is to protect their interests, and virtually every moment of their lives is spent in pursuit of this goal. Truth be told, no one is focused on anything else apart from this. Seen from this viewpoint, contemplation and deliberation seems to be the only right approach. In fact, there appears no other solution. However, this brings us back to the same question: if contemplation is so vital, why are people not able to protect their interests? Why is life mired in ever-new problems every day? Why isn't anyone receiving what they truly deserve? Indeed, these questions are repeatedly casting serious doubt on the process of contemplation and deliberation.

So, what should be done now that the process of contemplation and deliberation has begun to show cracks, especially when the alternative—acting spontaneously—seems uncertain and risky! Well, do not fret! If understood carefully, you'll see that in the course of an ordinary discussion we have arrived at one of the deepest and most profound questions surrounding *'karma'* (deeds): which of the two processes should be adopted to perform deeds—contemplation or spontaneity? And since life is nothing but a continuous chain of deeds, any question related to deeds is inherently a question about life itself.

From this perspective, we have stumbled upon one of the few, most significant questions about life. So, the more deeply you reflect on this, the more clarity and insight you will gain.

Well, the fundamental question still stands: is it better to perform deeds spontaneously or after careful deliberation? To answer this, let me first ask you something: Who possesses greater intelligence—you or Nature? Obviously Nature because, after all, Nature has been flawlessly orchestrating the universe for millennia, from the stars and the moon to the flow of the rivers and the sea, managing the rhythm of the seasons, the winds and countless other phenomena. I don't believe human intelligence can ever illuminate the sun or direct the course of winds with such perfection. Hence, it is futile to even compare 'Nature's intelligence' with man's ability to 'contemplate and deliberate'. I'm sure this point is clear to you, but you might still wonder: how does this relate to our lives? After all, it is we who have to manage our lives. Nature's intelligence does not help us in this matter. The stars and the moon are Nature's domain but we are tasked with managing our own lives. So, even if we admit that Nature's intelligence surpasses our own by a vast measure, how does it help us decide whether to perform deeds spontaneously or after deliberation?

This means the connection isn't obvious to you yet. So, let me explain. If Nature's intelligence governs the entire cosmos, why would it leave out its most precious creation—human beings? Why will it abandon us? It hasn't. In fact, it has gifted us with a remarkable tool, the 'spontaneous mind'. This spontaneous mind present within us is nothing but 'Nature's mind'. The science behind this is simple yet profound: instead of making decisions yourself, you have to entrust your decisions to Nature's mind. Instead of letting your brain engage in contemplations, you have to let Nature's mind engage in them. Without wasting a single moment, it promptly arrives at decisions that serve the best interest of all and also communicates those decisions to the human being's 'spontaneous mind'. And those who live spontaneously implement those decisions promptly as well. This is the very science of spontaneity. To fully understand this science, I urge you to read my book, 'I am The Mind'.

The most significant point to note is: Nature has not abandoned anyone, not even the tiniest speck in this vast expanse. It seeks the well-being of all, and in doing so, continuously makes decisions for every living entity at every moment of their lives. Moreover, it communicates these decisions with us through our spontaneous mind. Everything from intuition to sensing frequencies are wonders of the harmonious interplay between Nature's mind and the spontaneous mind. This naturally raises the question: why do people suppress such 'accurate spontaneous voices'? Simply because they have more faith in their own intellect. And here, the word 'faith' becomes paramount. In fact, the entire realm of psychology and spirituality is rooted in the word 'faith'. Both begin with 'faith in Nature' and even conclude at the same point. And those who have faith in Nature effortlessly engage in 'spontaneous deeds'.

Essentially, the world consists of two types of people: those who make most of their decisions spontaneously, and those who rely on deliberate, analytical thought for the majority of their decisions. And why does the latter group find it difficult to embrace spontaneity? The reason is either their ignorance of the spontaneous mind or a lack of trust in it. But understand clearly that lacking faith in your spontaneous mind implies you lack faith in Nature itself. This is precisely why all profound teachings of spirituality emphasise the importance of having

"If God exists, he certainly wants the best for you. And since he is looking after your best interests, why worry?

faith in Nature. I'm sure you too must have come across profound pearls of wisdom such as:

1. Do not burden yourself with worry; He is already looking out for you.
2. Whatever is happening, let it happen for therein lies your highest good.
3. With Allah's benevolence, even a pauper turns into a king.
4. Let Him decide your gains and losses, for His wisdom surpasses yours.
5. No harm can come to the one protected by Sai.
6. Listen to your inner voice—it will guide you in the right direction.

I'm certain that apart from the above-mentioned proverbs, you must have encountered various other spiritual principles too. In these proverbs, words such as Allah, Sai or He directly refer to your spontaneous mind or Nature's mind. And truly, nothing could be more beneficial than trusting this indication of Nature. Nevertheless, no matter how much I implore, you would still find it difficult to place complete faith in your spontaneous mind.

So, allow me to shed light on the interplay between spontaneous mind and Nature's mind and the phenomenal wonders they are capable of. Perhaps this reflection may rekindle your faith in spontaneity. Let me begin with a simple question: have you ever engaged in creativity? If yes, then you must have noticed how effortlessly it flows from within. This implies, creativity can only emerge spontaneously—it cannot flow through contemplation and deliberation. Try to create under pressure, with forced contemplation, and the result will often be uninspired. That kind of output will never reflect the profundity of Ghalib's poetry, the brilliance of Picasso's paintings, or the soul-stirring melodies of Naushad or Roshan. Why?

Because such depth can only come through the spontaneous mind, not from contemplation and deliberation. Therefore, everyone must grasp well the connection between creativity and spontaneous mind. It is also crucial to grasp that 'contemplation' and 'spontaneous mind' cannot be active simultaneously. No sooner does a person begin to contemplate than he instantly disconnects from his spontaneous mind. They are opposites, like east and west—two ends that can never meet. This essentially means that if spontaneity feels distant or dormant within you, it is only because 'the habit of contemplation' has become deeply entrenched. Seen from a spiritual perspective, it is this very habit of 'contemplation' that is not allowing you to 'connect with Nature'. This is precisely why those who make excessive use of their brain-intellect are never able to tap into their 'creative potential'. Because creativity can only emerge when you are in tune with Nature, and an excessive reliance on intellect becomes the greatest obstacle in aligning with Nature.

For now, let me ask you a question: what would you consider the two most extraordinary achievements in human history? The first is, undoubtedly, Einstein's discovery of the 'Theory of Relativity', and in case you are unaware, let me tell you, Einstein made this discovery spontaneously. This theory revolutionised science and changed our understanding of the universe; in fact, it wouldn't be erroneous to say that this theory is on par with Nature's intelligence. The second remarkable act is the enunciation of the Bhagavad Gita, an incredible wisdom that stemmed spontaneously from Krishna's consciousness. Krishna had no inkling that Arjuna would suddenly refuse to fight the Mahabharata war, compelling Krishna to enunciate the Gita. Yet, in that moment, Krishna spoke from a place so deep, so spontaneous, that the wisdom still resonates millennia later. And speaking of profundity, how can one forget the transcendental and thought-provoking dohās (verses) by the revered, mystic poet, Kabir. Every dohā emerged spontaneously from a man who did not even know how to read or write, which means he simply had no option to contemplate and deliberate at length while composing the dohās. So, ask yourself: if such great deeds can be accomplished without contemplation, why do we still cling to the belief that everything must be achieved through contemplation alone? Thus, from today onwards, pay close attention to spontaneity and spontaneous mind.

In case you are unaware, let me tell you that Einstein and Krishna—two of the most luminous figures in human history—lived their entire lives rooted in spontaneity. Take Krishna, for example. You may recall that he once vowed to Duryodhana that he would not take up arms during the Mahabharata war. And yet, at a pivotal moment, he did. Many accuse Krishna of breaking his vow, but such accusations arise only from a lack of psychological understanding, and Krishna would break a vow only if it was taken after careful contemplation. But Krishna was the embodiment of spontaneity, who lived spontaneously every second of his life. When he vowed not to wield weapons, he meant it fully in that moment. And later, when he did take up arms, he also meant that fully. To the contemplative mind, this seems contradictory because contemplation habitually connects the present with the past and the future; whereas in spontaneity, there is no past, future or present. Spontaneity is solely concerned with the deed at hand. For a spontaneous being, the vow given to Duryodhana was one action, and wielding the weapons was another action. For a spontaneous mind, there is absolutely no connection between these deeds. Thus, if viewed from this perspective, the notions of making a vow or breaking the said vow do not come into the picture at all. It is indeed sad to note that despite having scarce psychological and spiritual knowledge, people still want to comment on such matters. Who can make such people see that Krishna lived his life in a seamless flow! And for a person who lives in an effortless flow, there is no connection between 'two moments'. Such individuals live a new life every moment. Whichever action seems suitable in a particular moment in tune with time, circumstances and opportunity, they perform that action spontaneously. Hence, contemplation, deliberation, past, future, vows, blessings, curses and so on never come into play for them. This is why I say that it is not easy to understand either Krishna or spontaneity. And that is the reason why one has to label Krishna's actions as 'leela' (divine play) because his reasons for engaging in them are beyond one's comprehension. For this reason, I've written the entire psychological biography of Krishna in a comprehensive six-volume work titled 'I am Krishna'. Because only through psychological insight can one begin to understand the seamless, spontaneous flow in which he lived.

By now, you must have understood just how powerful the spontaneous mind is. And you have also probably realised that as long as you place more trust in contemplation and deliberation, your spontaneous mind will not be activated to its optimum capacity, and neither will you be able to truly trust its commands. This is the very peculiarity of spirituality. Though it is the ultimate science, placing unwavering faith in it or implementing it in life is far from easy. Wearing a tilak on the forehead, observing religious fasts or visiting places of worship is not difficult at all. But having absolute faith in Nature or God, however you name it, is exceedingly difficult. When you observe a fast or wear a tilak, you can at least convince yourself that you are religious. Even when you make a decision after careful thought, you can reassure yourself that you acted responsibly. But to act spontaneously and let Nature guide your choices? That feels uncertain—even risky.

I am well aware that transitioning to a life of spontaneity won't happen overnight. But I do hope that starting today, you will begin to pay attention to it, and as a first step, this is all I expect from you. There exists a world that is beyond constant thinking and contemplation, and I want to draw your attention towards that realm. And for that purpose, I am providing you a practical application. Use the chart below to make a note of all the major tasks you'll be undertaking over the next one month. Alongside each one, note whether you acted spontaneously or after careful thought. You are free to choose how you approach each task, but I suggest that in areas where you feel a little less apprehensive, try acting spontaneously. Later, reflect on the results. Compare the outcomes of the tasks done spontaneously with those done through contemplation. Fill in your observations in the space given in the chart. You will be surprised to find that all the deeds performed spontaneously are leading to positive outcomes.

Practical Application - A

No.	Deeds performed spontaneously	Describe the outcome of those deeds in detail
1.	....	....
2.	....	....
3.	....	....
4.	....	....
5.	....	....

Practical Application - B

No.	Deeds performed after due deliberation	Describe the outcome of those deeds
1.	....	....
2.	....	....

3.	....	....
4.	....	....
5.	....	....

Here, it is important to understand that there is a twist even when it comes to evaluating the 'outcome of deeds'. You perform a deed today but its results continue to unfold over an indefinite period. Take marriage, for example. Getting married is a one-day affair, but its impact stretches over a lifetime. So, unless the deed reaches its concluding point, it is difficult to fully evaluate its outcome. And this isn't limited to marriage. Many actions bring immediate joy or success, but eventually make us realise the repercussions of the problem we have got ourselves tangled in. At the time of wedding, everyone feels that they're on top of the world, but as time passes by, reality sets in and what once felt like a blessing starts to feel like a burden. This is precisely why it is not easy to evaluate the outcome of a deed. What's worse, outcomes don't arrive all at once—they unfold gradually, and often, indefinitely.

But even so, people often speak of "love at first sight". And yes, such love exists but only when one falls in love at first sight without prior thought or consideration. Because this kind of love is spontaneous, and often brings more peace and joy compared to the love you find after matching horoscopes or considering social status. But again, you must not forget that the outcome of deeds continues to unfold indefinitely. Over time, what seemed like a blessing can become a struggle, and what looked like a mistake can reveal unexpected blessings. It does not take long for gains to turn into losses, and losses into gains. Given this, the human brain simply cannot predict or calculate the final outcome of a deed. Imagine you started a new business and made a profit of ₹4 crore (40 million rupees) in the first four years. Naturally, you would consider starting this business a good decision. But then, in the fifth year, you suffer a massive loss of ₹10 crore (100 million rupees). Now tell me—would you still call that initial decision a good one? This is precisely why I say, the human intellect has limited capacity to assess whether an action was ultimately good or bad. This is why even after extensive deliberation, the balance sheet of life reveals more losses than gains.

You might find this statement unsettling, and perhaps even wonder if I've written this book to eliminate confusion or worsen it. But let me reassure you: my goal is to relieve you of confusion. And to do that, I must conduct a psychoanalysis of every aspect of this subject. Because not only is this subject far more complex than it may seem at first glance, but it also holds within it the ultimate secret of Nature. Although this book isn't about spontaneity, I want you to have at least a fair idea about the power of spontaneity. And in that context, understand clearly that whether a deed is performed through spontaneity or contemplation, both approaches ultimately pertain to 'action'. No matter which approach you take, your actions must produce a favourable result. But that leads to the bigger question: how do we ascertain whether the deed was beneficial or not? Because deeds, by their very nature, produce results that unfold perpetually, until the end of time. Besides, a deed sometimes leads to a 'sour' experience while at other times brings a 'sweet' experience. This being the case, it becomes

Superficial thoughts cannot make a person smile on the gallows like Bhagat Singh. For that, the fire of patriotism must burn bright in 'experience'

challenging to deduce with our ordinary intelligence what the actual outcome of a deed is.

This leads to yet another question: how should life's decisions be made? How should we analyse our deeds? Oh! Have you not figured it out yet? The answer lies in faith and only faith! The best way to live is to have complete 'faith in Nature'. If great people like Krishna and Einstein could ascend to such heights by placing their faith in Nature, why can't we? Let me ask you this: since you contemplate and deliberate so much, can you come up with a solution that is better than the one that proposes placing faith in Nature? Neither is your brain equipped with a vision like Nature's, nor does it possess such vast intelligence. So, why burden it with questions like: What should I do? What will benefit me the most? This constant tug-of-war only leads to confusion. A spontaneous mind connected with Nature already resides within you, so let your deeds stem from its womb without thinking or contemplation. This is the best approach, because we now know that the outcomes of deeds continue to unfold indefinitely. We are also aware that in the realm of deeds, it takes only a split second for 'gains' to turn into 'losses' and vice-versa. In other words, it is not easy to determine which deeds would guarantee a better outcome, because it is impossible to analyse the outcome of deeds. So, why contemplate on anything? Act as per the guidance of your spontaneous mind and allow whatever happens to just happen. Trust completely that Nature has guided you to act, so whatever happens eventually will turn out for the best. I guarantee, anyone who elevates himself to this pinnacle of spirituality will live a magnificent life. I state this with utmost conviction, because I am well acquainted with this science and it has undeniably shaped my own life.

If you truly wish to free yourself from confusion, you must embrace the essence of the highest prayer in spirituality: a quiet, unwavering surrender to Nature. Ask yourself honestly: what is the true range of my understanding or the extent of my knowledge? What power do I truly hold to secure my welfare? So, here's my earnest advice: let go and surrender to Nature. Go with what Nature urges you to do and have faith that whatever has transpired, whatever is transpiring and whatever will transpire will happen for your ultimate good. Consider yourself spiritual only once you are able to follow this or inch closer to it. Comprehend the simple fact that while contemplation is necessary to determine which deeds must be performed, the vital question is: who should be the one contemplating—you or Nature? The entire game of life rests on this single decision. Truth be told, this is the only decision you have to make. But you are the kind of genius who expertly avoids the one decision that actually matters, and instead makes a thousand utterly pointless ones. But now, the time has come for you to determinedly make this decision. And only if you select 'Nature' in this decision, should you nurture 'grand expectations' from yourself. When Buddha abandoned his royal comforts, it was not a calculated decision. It was spontaneous. Even his decision to embark on the quest of truth was a spontaneous one. He did not pause to wonder, who will care for my wife and child or what will become of me? Had he hesitated, he would have never been able to leave the palace. And just see, the spontaneous decision he made without contemplation led him on the path of becoming the 'great Buddha'! Had he stayed in the palace, would anyone even know his name today? There were many princes hailing from much larger and reputed kingdoms back then, but have you ever heard of any of them?

This is why I urge you to recognise the vast, incredible intelligence of Nature and the extraordinary power of spontaneity. Of course, you won't become spontaneous overnight, but at the very least, start paying attention to it. Understand that there is another way to act, beyond contemplation-deliberation. I agree, you will not become spontaneous overnight because the entire game of spontaneity is about 'having complete faith in Nature' and this faith will take root only gradually. But you will be able to place faith in Nature only when you take the first step! And it is crucial to have faith in Nature and its spontaneity because when everything in Nature lives in a seamless 'flow', just like the wind and water, your life should also flow effortlessly. Comprehend well that thoughts imply obstruction; and obstruction gives rise to confusion, which leads to unnecessary problems. Despite this, one cannot let go of one's habit of contemplation. In any case, no principle of spirituality is ever easy to abide by, and that is precisely why, carving a great life is no cakewalk either. Let's take spontaneity for instance. If you wish to embrace spontaneity, you will have to forsake thoughts about the past and future. You will have to relinquish worries concerning your betterment. And these are no easy tasks! But do not forget this will all be possible only once you take the first step in this direction.

Now, whether this path feels simple or challenging, I've shared with you the ultimate solution to eliminate confusion. Once you start living spontaneously, confusion will never hold you in its grip; there is no other solution to find a complete respite from confusion. However, this does not mean you should stop using your intellect or avoid all contemplation. Please do not misconstrue my words. Contemplation, thought and analysis have their own place. After all, if contemplation was useless, Nature wouldn't have gifted you with a brain capable of it. All I'm emphasising is that when it comes to decision-making i.e. selection, the choice must be made spontaneously. The decision of which data to consider and which to discard must be made spontaneously. The rest of the process, from analysing the 'data' to implementing the deed, has to be done through careful deliberation only. So, understand that we are discussing decision-making and selection, not analysis, management or implementation. Besides, know well that you are riddled with confusion not in the implementation, but in the selection of the deed. And that is why I urge you—whenever possible, make your decisions spontaneously. To explain this from a spiritual perspective, allow Nature to make decisions i.e. allow your spontaneous mind to make decisions and then implement them using your intellect. This is the very tuning between Nature and the human being that everyone must strive to achieve.

If the idea still feels a bit unclear, allow me to clarify with a simple example. Imagine you are choosing a career, let's say in science. The decision to become a scientist should stem from an all-consuming, passionate desire within you i.e. spontaneously—similar to Edison who took the spontaneous decision of becoming a scientist despite limited education and the penurious state of his family. Something inside him burned with the desire to become a scientist, and he followed that instinct without hesitation. Had he sat down to logically analyse his circumstances, doubt would have crept in, making him wonder, "How can someone like me with no resources or education become a scientist?" That kind of thinking would have stopped him before he even began. In fact, contemplation-deliberation would have cautioned him with the thought that becoming a scientist is a very expensive pursuit. 'In such dire financial circumstances wherein it is virtually impossible to even afford our daily bread, how can we decide to become a scientist?' However, since Edison was spontaneous, he took the decision of becoming a scientist. Of course, once the decision was made, he did use contemplation and deliberation to chart his course. And that is exactly how it should be. You can decide to get married spontaneously, but planning the wedding definitely requires some thinking! So, don't confuse the two. Spontaneity and contemplation are two entirely different processes, and both are equally useful. For, although the decision comes from Nature, you're the one who has to act on it, right? Simply put, let Nature show you what to do, and you figure out how to do it. And since Nature is not teaching you 'how to do things', you too must not explain to Nature 'what must be done'. Once you awaken this understanding, your life will soar to unprecedented heights. The crux of the matter is, allow decisions to happen spontaneously as far as possible, and let your contemplation-deliberation be restricted only to their implementation. Spontaneity does not mean that contemplation has no place in your life. Contemplation-deliberation has its own place, but let the direction of life be defined by spontaneity.

There is one more important truth you need to understand clearly: spontaneity is your very 'life-force'. It is just that you do not have enough self-awareness or adequate knowledge about psychology or spirituality. But the fact is that spontaneity is a gift from Nature itself, which is why it is so closely connected to you. It is due to your habit of excessive thinking as well as external pressures that you have become totally disconnected from your own 'life-force'. In other words, you may well be breathing, but you are devoid of your essential 'life-force'. And sadly, most people don't even realise this. Frankly speaking, it pains me greatly to witness this sheer ignorance of psychology. Let me give you a small insight: your mood too is closely linked to spontaneity. You could even say that mood is spontaneity's younger sibling. And you know from experience that it's hard to even talk to someone when they're in a bad mood. Now think about this: if the younger sibling is so powerful, how powerful the elder sibling—spontaneity—must be! Given this, one can only imagine the consequences of acting against spontaneity. In essence, both mood and spontaneity are nothing but a 'natural flow'. Both are boons bestowed by Nature. If you are interested in exploring this deeply, read my book 'I am Time' in which you will uncover the ultimate secret of the power of spontaneity. Now, this doesn't mean that contemplation is powerless. Not at all! Both spontaneity and contemplation are powerful in their own right, but they work in different ways and serve different purposes. Here's a simple example: the craving for pani puri (a popular Indian snack) arises spontaneously, but deciding where to eat it, which vendor to trust, and how spicy you want it to be are decisions that require thinking. So, don't confuse the two.

As per the design of Nature, a human being can carve a magnificent life for himself only on the strength of his deeds. Deeds are the very foundation of human life. On this point, there should be no confusion. But the real question is: what should be the basis of performing deeds? The answer is simple—deeds should 'flow' naturally, because all deeds in Nature occur in a smooth, uninterrupted flow. Nature's arrangement is such that the moment there is a disruption in the flow of your deeds, you deviate from your destination. So, why does this flow get disrupted? The sole reason is confusion. Confusion puts deeds on hold. It creates hesitation, making you question, "Should I do this or that?" And when you're stuck in indecision, nothing gets done. Whereas, it is the continuity of deeds that provides flow to life. That is why confusion is such a serious roadblock to progress. So, kindly do not take it lightly.

Now, everyone wants their deeds to lead to positive outcomes, and for that, every person will have to consider their benefit and accordingly choose an option that is correct and positive. All these points are valid but you can't arrive at the best decision through contemplation-deliberation, because contemplation and deliberation imply confusion regarding which option to select. The alternative then is spontaneous decision-making, which means entrusting the decision to Nature and refraining from applying your intellect. We have grasped that there are two ways to carve a grand existence: one by trying to figure out your benefit yourself, and two, by placing your trust in Nature's intelligence. Each one of us has a spontaneous mind dwelling within us which is directly connected to Nature. And because it draws from that vast intelligence, it is far more powerful than our own intelligence. It can make the right decision in an instant. And naturally, when decisions are made in a split second, the flow of deeds will never be disrupted. This implies a confusion-free life! This is the kind of seamless flow you see in the lives of the truly great, be it Krishna or Einstein. You can live like that too, provided you put a tight leash on needless contemplations and deliberations! However, it is not easy to rein in this habit. For that purpose, rather than 'worrying about your own benefit', you will have to entrust your worries to Nature, because only then can you flow spontaneously. Otherwise, excessive thinking and confusion will keep swarming into your life and obstruct its natural flow.

In short, spontaneity is only possible when you place unwavering trust in the intelligence and intentions of Nature. And please do not tread this path unless 'you have complete faith in Nature', otherwise you will find yourself in deeper quagmires. Just as lending money to someone you don't trust robs you of peace of mind, if you start making decisions spontaneously without first 'placing your faith in Nature or the spontaneous mind', you will find yourself wandering aimlessly in a state of bewilderment. Therefore, do not rush. To even understand the science of spontaneity and recognising its significance is a good start; the rest will unfold in its own time. I am not a motivational speaker who pushes one towards reckless confidence. My purpose is to unravel the mysteries of spirituality and psychology. So, take deliberate, thoughtful steps. Begin with small, low-risk actions carried out spontaneously. As your faith deepens, expand the scope of your deeds. Eventually, a time will come when you will entrust all your worries to Nature, allowing your spontaneous mind to make the significant decisions of your life. Such a day will surely dawn into your life provided you continue to sharpen your psychological insight and awaken your spiritual understanding. 'True spirituality' is ultimately surrendering your worries to Nature. Everything else you hear and read about is just folklore and mythical stories in the garb of spirituality. But remember, a great life is built not from fables and stories, but from truths rooted in spirituality. I have pointed you in the right direction, so walk the path step by step and life will begin to flow effortlessly, just like water or the drift of the wind.

In essence, the fog of confusion can be cut through only with 'flow', and this flow arises from the spontaneous mind alone, because it is brimming with the intelligence of Nature. This is why the spontaneous mind is not riddled with confusion regarding deeds, because it understands that no action yields only good, positive outcomes. Therefore, the spontaneous mind will instantly choose the deed that results in a greater good and lesser bad. It knows when to listen to the mind and when to heed the brain-ego, because it functions like a supercomputer—far more powerful, precise and attuned than the brain-ego could ever be. The real question is: can you trust it? Can you place unwavering faith in the intelligence and power of Nature? That trust will arise only when you stop 'worrying about yourself'. So, stop worrying and embrace spontaneity. Then watch how effortlessly your life begins to flow and confusion starts to dissolve simultaneously. Remember, any disruption in the flow of life is nothing but a sin. Confusion is a sin and so is putting deeds on pause. Once you recognise this, start purging yourself of these sins on a daily basis. With every release, your life will soar higher. Consider all other notions of 'sin' you may have heard or read about as nothing more than fiction. I'm speaking with absolute clarity and conviction, so let these words sink in. It brings me great solace to know that those of you who once relied solely on contemplation-deliberation have now come to grasp the science of spontaneity. And make no mistake: even this understanding marks a profound turning point in your life, because from this day on, you are going to continuously observe your spontaneity, and that very observation will keep aligning you with Nature.

Be Content

in What You Receive Naturally

In the Bhagavad Gita, Krishna offers a powerful antidote to confusion. Speaking to Arjuna, he declares, "O Arjuna, the one who remains perpetually content with what he receives naturally, remains content forever." In this simple yet profound statement, Krishna reveals the ultimate truth of Nature. Let us explore the profundity of this verse. When a human being arrives in this world, he comes empty-handed, carrying nothing but the rhythm of his heartbeat. And from that point onwards, he must navigate the entire journey of life and traverse myriad pathways to 'attain' countless things in this world, be it material comforts, wealth, relationships, skills—all must be drawn from the vast reservoir of life. But this leads us to a deeper question: who or what should determine what a person must attain?

Today, it is the individual who decides. First, he determines what he wishes to attain and then makes efforts to fulfil those desires. Indeed, the vast majority follows this process of performing deeds. I'm sure this pattern is clear to you. But Krishna proposes a radically different approach. He proclaims, 'Be content in whatever you receive 'effortlessly' during the natural course of life.' In other words, do not insist on determining what you want. However, this raises a pertinent question: if we do not determine what we want, how will we perform deeds? And how will we attain anything if we don't perform deeds?

If this question has crossed your mind, I'm sad to say that you have no idea about Nature's *leela* (the play of Nature), spirituality or even psychology. Honestly, this is not a good sign at all.

Now, the question arises: why does the puny human ego presume that he alone must determine everything? Why cling to the illusion that unless 'I' take charge, nothing will happen? Even Nature, which orchestrates the entire universe, does not suffer from such arrogance. Ask yourself: how will things work out if you keep acting this way? So, cultivate and sharpen your psychological insight and make an earnest effort to fathom the profundity of matters. Do not wander through life blindfolded by arrogance and ignorance. When a supreme consciousness like Krishna speaks, at least pay heed to what he says.

This brings us back to the main issue—the ignorance surrounding 'psycho-spirituality'. And it is this very lack of understanding that leads people to believe they must decide everything they want to extract from the reservoir of life. That they alone must chart the course of what to pursue to shape a spectacular life. The irony, however, is striking—not only do most people 'fail to attain' what they chase, but even when they do, it does not bring them true 'joy'. And yet, the ego persists, clinging to the belief that if we don't take charge, life will somehow stop functioning. Why does this delusion persist? It is only because until one determines what one wishes to attain, one is unable to engage in deeds. In other words, in order to perform a 'deed', it is crucial to first determine what you wish to attain from that deed. This means it is impossible to engage in a deed without the expectations of fruits. But Krishna, in the Gita, offers a radically different insight which says, 'Perform your deed, but do not harbour expectations of its fruits.' That is, perform your deeds without harbouring any expectations concerning its results. But surprisingly, no one knows how to do this. This implies, people worship Krishna but do not pay heed to his words. And that, tragically, is what religiousness has come to mean for many today. And with a world filled with such superficial religiosity, both religion and Krishna will certainly be doomed.

For now, try to grasp your core problem. Your primary issue remains your ignorance about psychology and spirituality, and it is this ignorance that compels you to believe that nothing will ever transpire unless you yourself determine it. It is this very ignorance which leaves you incapable of performing deeds without deciding first. Consequently, you end up believing that to attain anything, there exists only one process—first determine what you desire, then perform deeds and finally achieve what you desire. This implies, if you do not determine anything, you will never be able to attain anything. And if you actually follow this line of thinking, then tread with extreme caution because this thought process is entirely wrong. Moreover, when Krishna himself corroborates this, it is undeniably the absolute truth. Because he is, after all, the ultimate master of psychology and spirituality.

So, first, comprehend well that you don't need to determine every single thing. Second, etch it in your mind that you don't have to engage in deeds with the sole intent of achieving something. At the same time, get rid of the misconception that if you don't determine things, you will not achieve anything. The truth of the matter is, 'Nature' desires your benefit and well-being more than you do yourself. Furthermore, it possesses 'power and intelligence' that surpasses your own by a million-fold. I'm sure you don't doubt this for a second. So, why not place your faith in Nature? When it desires your benefit, possesses far greater intelligence and power than you, then let it determine what

Clear the path for your most cherished desires—remove what obstructs and welcome what supports. You'll never be confused again

you must receive. Have faith that your benefit lies in that alone. But yes, if you have doubts about Nature's 'intention', then it is a different matter.

Well, I hope after giving such a detailed explanation, your faith in Nature must have strengthened to some extent. In any case, if you worship Krishna, your faith in Nature must surely be unwavering. But the problem is, although you worship Krishna, you don't really believe in him. But now, start believing too...! Because you will be able to carve a remarkable life not by 'worshipping' Krishna, but by 'believing' in his words. So now, I am proceeding with the assumption that you have placed some faith in Nature. And if you have, then allow it to determine what you deserve to achieve. If you find it hard to vest complete faith in all areas of your life, have faith in some areas at least. The key is to make a start somewhere!

So, let us proceed with the premise that you have faith in Nature. But I'm sure this will prompt another question in your mind: 'How will I know what Nature has ordained for me? How will Nature communicate with me?' As mentioned earlier, Nature will communicate with you through your 'spontaneous mind', which is wirelessly connected with Nature. This is precisely why it holds immense significance. Thus, as soon as you start having 'faith in Nature', your spontaneous mind will become active. Thereafter, you will receive regular messages from Nature regarding 'which deeds you must perform'. And by heeding the command of the spontaneous mind, if you continue to perform those deeds, you will automatically start attaining everything that Nature has ordained for you. Moreover, since Nature's power and intelligence are unparalleled, you will not only continue to receive the finest of everything, but you will also start attaining it at a faster pace. And needless to say, only those who can implement this in their lives will achieve remarkable progress. Viewed from this perspective, it is evident that without activating the spontaneous mind and without tuning oneself with Nature, no human being can attain unprecedented success. Unfortunately, since only a small percentage of people is able to do this, the world is rife with failures.

I hope you have now grasped the essence of both the verses enunciated by Krishna as well as the indication given by him. Whatever you receive as a result of the decisions made by the spontaneous mind is termed as 'received naturally'. This is because in those decisions, you have not determined 'what needs to be achieved'. Comprehend well that the deeds are performed by you, and you certainly reap the fruits of your actions—the only difference is, the decision pertaining to the selection of the deeds is taken by the spontaneous mind. Therefore, do not mistakenly assume that simply by going to the Himalayas and meditating in solitude, you will attain everything. I am compelled to make such clarifications because human 'intelligence' cannot be trusted at all! And now that we are on the subject, I must address one more point. Those who are familiar with this spiritual science carry just one prayer on their lips day and night—'Let your will be fulfilled, for what is the scope of my intelligence to be able to discern what is good for me. Let your blessings be showered upon me, for what power do I have to attain anything?' And if you too wish to tune yourself with Nature, say this prayer as soon as you wake up every morning. This prayer will strengthen your faith in Nature and weaken your habit of determining things. Additionally, it will also teach you to perform 'deeds' without harbouring any expectations of results. Basically, this prayer will work like a magic pill! Note carefully: I am suggesting that you entrust all the decisions pertaining to which actions you must perform and what you must attain to Nature. However, all the subsequent tasks after the decision is made have to be executed by you with the help of your mind, brain and ego. To that end, Nature will not extend its support to you. Therefore, never try to go against the 'science of *karma*'. We are not talking about abandoning the world and embracing renunciation—we are discussing the science of achieving great success.

In conclusion, comprehend one more important point: it is not that you completely lack faith in Nature or you perform all your actions only after 'determining' them yourself. And neither is it the case that you are totally oblivious to the approach of performing deeds 'without the expectation of fruits'. What I mean to say is, you are not absolutely clueless about the 'science of spontaneity'. In many instances, you have surely engaged in deeds in a focused and concentrated state of mind, but since your focus and concentration were not intense enough, you were unaware of it. But believe me, knowingly or unknowingly, everyone has invariably placed their faith in Nature countless times. And if you want proof, just peek into your own life. I'm sure you must be having in your possession a vast number of things that include material possessions, relationships, talents, hobbies, habits, etc. Now, I request you to take a moment and sit in solitude and reflect: Had you consciously decided to achieve all of these? The answer will astonish you because you will find countless things in your possession that you had never even imagined attaining. Just think, when you had never even imagined acquiring those things, how did they come into your life? From various hobbies and habits to numerous belongings and relationships, these are possessions you never actually intended to have. So, please don't ask how anything can be gained on its own without determining it. You have already attained a multitude of things 'effortlessly' without planning for them.

Once you come to the realisation that you have received countless things without consciously desiring or determining them, don't let that insight go in vain. Conduct a sincere and honest introspection of your

You can accomplish anything you desire—but remember, you cannot 'go against your own nature' even if you wish to

life thus far and examine: of all the possessions and experiences in your life, how many have come as a result of consciously desiring, and how many have arrived without any desire on your part? Do not take this exercise lightly. Remember, rarely does life present such a brilliant opportunity to eliminate confusion and 'connect with Nature'. If you ignore this, you may not get another chance like it. Now, after assessing the balance sheet of your life, you'll find that you possess countless things that you had never desired. So, what does this mean? Well, the insights gained will reveal the following points:

- **You are not entirely disconnected from Nature. On numerous occasions, you have certainly been in tune with Nature.**
- **The belief that you are the sole architect of your life is a misconception. Often, you have followed Nature's guidance, perhaps unknowingly.**
- **The idea that you cannot perform deeds without harbouring expectations of fruits is also false. Time and again, you have performed deeds without any expectation of fruits.**
- **Most importantly, it is not as if you won't attain anything without desiring or determining it. You have often gained many things without desiring or determining them.**

This reflection ignites a new sense of hope for both you and me. And now that you have this deeper understanding, I encourage you to go a step further: you know you possess two categories of things—those you desired and those you didn't—so ask yourself which ones have truly brought you joy. Once again, you will be surprised. The things you have gained without desiring are providing greater happiness in life, while the majority of the possessions you have gained after desiring and determining have brought disappointment or sorrow. This clearly shows, what Nature has ordained for you is proving to be far more beneficial for you than what you have determined for yourself. I don't think this point needs further elaboration, so gradually, let go of the habit of determining things for yourself and start entrusting your decisions to Nature.

Now, while you have grasped all these insights, our main subject—confusion—still remains our priority. And in that context, understand well that confusion will persist as long as 'you' are determining things. When you try to determine what's best for you, you are forced to contemplate over choices, outcomes and expectations. That is where confusion arises. But when Nature determines for you, you are relieved of that burden. In other words, there is no room for confusion. This implies, 'Be content with what you receive naturally' and 'Perform your deeds, but do not harbour expectations of fruits' are the ultimate solutions to triumph over confusion. This is precisely why I have emphasised them so strongly. So, grasp them in their entirety and secure victory over confusion; once you do so, I'll know that my effort has been worthwhile.

The Essence

We have explored in depth the causes, effects and solutions for freeing ourselves from confusion. But given the gravity and profundity of this subject, it is better to summarise our discussion through a fresh perspective. Evidently, there exists a perpetual flow in all the deeds of Nature. Whether it is the sun rising, the wind blowing, the rivers flowing or any other element in Nature, the seamless flow of their deeds has never ceased. Since human beings are also an inseparable part of Nature, if they too wish to reach their destination, the flow of their deeds should never cease. But as we have seen, this is not happening, and consequently, humans are unable to reach their destination. In fact, the failure to reach one's destination is the fundamental reason behind humans 'going astray'. Sorrow, stress, fear, frustration and all other negative emotions arise only because one deviates from one's path.

This brings us to an essential question: If all the deeds in Nature occur in a perpetual flow, what is holding humans back? The answer is vital because it lies at the heart of why we lose our way. Here, it is also essential to note that since 'the causes behind all the problems afflicting human life' lie hidden in the secrets of Nature, the solutions will also have to be found in Nature itself. It also goes without saying that since human beings are ignorant of the secrets of Nature, they are unable to find solutions to any of their problems. Truth be told, this very ignorance about psychology and spirituality is costing human beings dearly. Otherwise, human life lived with grace and splendour can make even Nature envy its magnificence. And you must live such a spectacular life! But to do so, remember that there must be a continuous 'flow in your deeds'. This brings us back to the same question: why are human beings unable to perform deeds in a flow? The sole reason is confusion because it repeatedly hinders the flow of deeds; and there is no denying the fact that everyone is paralysed by confusion in almost every matter.

The only reason people are mired in so much confusion is because of their ignorance of Nature's laws. Human desires, rooted in ignorance, clash with the laws of Nature and give birth to confusion. People fail to grasp the fundamental truth that you cannot override the laws of Nature. You may think you can, but this very 'thinking' gives rise to numerous confusions. For instance, very few people are aware that everything in Nature exists in a state of 'balance'. And *karma* and its fruits are no exception to this. *Karma* and its fruits are balanced on the scale of 'gains-losses and good-bad'. So, regardless of the deed performed, it will inevitably comprise both gain and loss or good and bad. Yet, unaware of this supreme law, people seek to engage in deeds that would bring only gains and good outcomes. But this is impossible as per Nature's law. So, when they fear the potential for loss or any sort of negativity, they put the deed on pause. And in doing so, they interrupt the 'flow of deeds'. We have already grasped this in our psychoanalysis. I'm reiterating it here so that its essence is etched in your mind forever. So, let me re-emphasise: if you truly wish to be free of confusion, stop fearing 'losses and bad outcomes'. Continue to perform deeds that entail a greater amount of gain and good and lesser amount of loss and bad. This is the only solution to free yourself from the clutches of confusion. Because in this vast realm of Nature, it is simply impossible to perform a deed that does not involve some amount of loss or produce a bad outcome.

Later on in our discussion, we also understood that Nature has sent us into this world with a limited "basket" of everything. Therefore, if our desires begin to exceed the limits of this basket, confusion will obviously arise. We have also grasped that although human beings possess the ability to do anything, we cannot act against our own nature. Therefore, if we truly wish to safeguard ourselves from confusion, we must refrain from acting against our 'three core desires'. Because as per the design of Nature, man can do anything he desires, but he cannot act against himself. Yet, compelled by external pressures, influences and helplessness, he ends up doing precisely that and finds himself trapped. Consequently, his behaviour becomes confusing and such behaviour is no less dangerous than confusion itself.

Through this book, we have delved into a profound psychological discussion about confusion, its causes and remedies. The causes we have discussed are the very reasons why human beings fall into confusion. By addressing and eliminating them, you can minimise your confusions significantly. Of course, apart from this, you may have come across many other viewpoints on the subject of confusion; and verily, there is no dearth of people who claim that "confusion is bad". But what purpose does it serve to merely label something as bad? The discussion must be focused on the solution; lamenting over the problem is frankly speaking a foolish exercise. Likewise, indulging in empty, motivational slogans such as, "Wake up and dispel the dark clouds of confusion!" or "You're human, you can do anything!" cannot be called a sign of intelligence either. The truth is, comprehending any aspect about

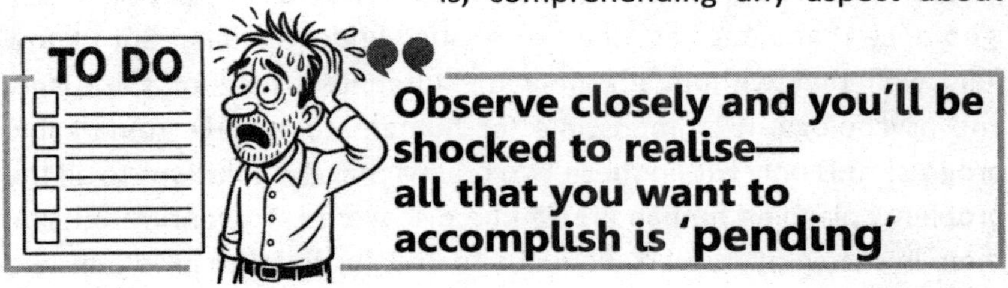

TO DO

Observe closely and you'll be shocked to realise— all that you want to accomplish is 'pending'

the human being is impossible without an in-depth psychoanalysis. And by performing a detailed psychoanalysis, we have grasped all the main causes of confusion. Never before has this subject been addressed in such clarity and detail, and that, in itself, marks a meaningful step forward.

As we progressed further in our discussion, we came to a pivotal realisation: man has been grappling with confusion only because his efforts are aimed in a direction that is contrary to the design of Nature. This further led us to discover solutions to alleviate confusion. Then came the question: can one truly find total respite from confusion? Can a person spend his entire life free of confusion? Most would hesitate to answer 'yes' to this question. However, through our in-depth psychoanalysis, we also discovered solutions to live a confusion-free life. There are three definitive ways: One, if a person lives with a single purpose, his confusions will be eliminated to a large extent. Two, if a person lives spontaneously, he will triumph over confusion in an instant. Three, if a person learns to be content in whatever he receives effortlessly, he will surely liberate himself from all confusions forever. These are the only three methods to completely rid oneself of confusion and we have discovered all three of them. In fact, we have not just discovered them, but have also fathomed their spiritual significance in depth. Anyone who earnestly embraces even one of these paths will undoubtedly reach their destination, because then their deeds will flow seamlessly without any interruption. In fact, all those who have left a lasting mark on this world—those luminous figures we call great—have walked one of these very paths. It is only psychological ignorance that stands as a barrier to such understanding. But I know fully well that without grasping the ultimate truths of spirituality and psychology, it is impossible for humans to achieve remarkable progress. It is only within these two realms that the solutions to all the problems plaguing human life can be discovered. To venture outside them in search of answers would be to drift further into problems and lose sight of the path back entirely. Take this as a sincere suggestion or even a gentle warning—but do not ignore it.

Most significantly, after all these in-depth explanations, you must start taking a genuine interest in spiritual and psychological discussions and, based on their solutions, actively work on overcoming all your confusions. But if neither of these occurs—if interest does not awaken and confusion continues—then somewhere, a lapse must have occurred either in your efforts or mine. Even so, I shall not stop.

I will continue, steadfast and unwavering, to dispel the clouds of ignorance. One by one, I will examine the deeper roots of all the problems that afflict human life, and through careful psychoanalysis, I will strive to illuminate the path forward.

With heartfelt gratitude!

Deep Trivedi